$\mathscr{S}$IMPLY
$\mathscr{D}$IVINE

SIMPLY DIVINE

200 Inspired (and Effortless) Desserts

Rita M. Harris

PRIMA PUBLISHING

PRIMA PUBLISHING and colophon are trademarks of Prima Communications, Inc.

Library of Congress Cataloging-in-Publication Data

Harris, Rita M.
    Simply divine: 200 inspired (and effortless) desserts / by Rita M. Harris.
      p.   cm.
    Includes index.
    ISBN 0-7615-0300-5
    1. Desserts   2. Quick and easy cookery.   I. Title.
    TX773.H317   1995
641.8'6—dc20   95-33229
                                                CIP

95 96 97 98 99 DD 10 9 8 7 6 5 4 3 2 1
Printed in the United States of America

How to Order:

Single copies may be ordered from Prima Publishing, P.O. Box 1260BK, Rocklin, CA 95677; telephone (916) 632-4400. Quantity discounts are also available. On your letterhead, include information concerning the intended use of the books and the number of books you wish to purchase.

Lust for Chocolate

by Daniel Will-Harris

Did you know that the original Ten Commandments were actually ten chocolate recipes?

Moses had ascended a high mountain in order to communicate with God. God handed Moses two chocolate tablets on which were inscribed the recipes for ten fabulous chocolate desserts. Moses stopped when he saw the burning bush just long enough for the heat to cause the chocolate to melt a little. Moses licked his fingers and he was hooked! He broke off a section of the tablet and ate it.

Then he remembered the roaring crowd at the base of the mountain awaiting his return from his meeting with God.

He couldn't remember the exact proportions of the recipes and was afraid that there would be panic when things didn't bake correctly. In his attempt to restore order and create peace, he came up with the Ten Commandments as we know them today and quickly chiseled them on two stone tablets he found on the mountain.

Of course the chocolate recipes would probably have worked better because they were, after all, simply divine!

Contents

Acknowledgments

This book is dedicated to my loyal Humboldt County, California, fans as well as to those far beyond the Redwood Curtain. It was your encouragement and support that enabled me to teach myself to bake when I was 52 years old. You helped me develop something new in the bakery business and it's flattering that a number of bakeries have copied my designs.

The little dessert parlor in Arcata and the bakery in Old Town Eureka are both memories, but our truffles, cakes, cheesecakes, and elegant desserts, introduced by Chocoholics Bakery and Chocoholics Dessert Parlor in 1979, are still remembered by many. You asked for my recipes and here they are. Many ingredients we used, such as cocoas, are only available in commercial sizes, so I have substituted cake mixes here. Wherever possible I have simplified the recipes making them simply divine! Enjoy.

My thanks to my partner, pal, and best friend Bill Wintroub, whose encouragement and patience in teaching me to use a computer merit an award. He has been my strongest advocate and my gratitude to him is endless. This book is especially dedicated to my children, Lisa and Loren Skyhorse, Howard and Catherine Harris, and Daniel and Toni Will-Harris. And, of course, to my grandchildren, Ocea, Ari, Richard, and Alexander: thanks for the memories!

My special thanks to my son Daniel for his "Lust For Chocolate." And of course, my gratitude to Prima Publishing, Alice Anderson, Acquisitions Editor, and Debra Venzke, Project Editor, for their support.

The Baker Is In

As you look through the following pages of divine desserts, I hope you'll find many old favorites as well as some new ones to add to your culinary repertoire.

As you bake, if you have any questions or suggestions, I'd love to hear from you. I can be reached at:

Rita M. Harris
Post Office Box 890
Trinidad, California 95570
Fax: 707/677-3405

If you would like more information on Chocoholics ChocolateButter, call 800/760-CHOC. It's available in both traditional and fat-free varieties.

As a final note, every baker is particularly fond of certain recipes. To indicate my personal favorites, a small cherub illustration is placed alongside the recipes. *Bon appétit!*

INGREDIENTS FOR DIVINE DESSERTS

As a baker, I am frequently asked for definitions and explanations about ingredients. I have finally compiled the answers to some of the most commonly asked questions. The more you know about ingredients, the better baker you will be!

Cream

Light Cream

Used for coffee or in recipes where a certain richness is desired; contains about 20 percent butterfat and will not whip.

Heavy Whipping Cream

Heavy whipping cream contains 36 to 40 percent butterfat, making it ideal for ice cream and frostings. Chill the bowl, cream, and beater before beating. Always beat the cream until frothy before adding the sugar. If you are using large quantities to frost a wedding cake or lots of cakes at one time, purchase heavy manufacturing cream from a dairy.

Sour Cream

Commercially cultured light cream that is thick and tangy. It is used to give a zesty flavor and richness. Also available in lowfat and fat-free.

Eggs

Used to thicken custards and add a light texture to batters and doughs, as well as a binding agent in baked goods. The recipes in this book use large and extra-large eggs.

To make eggs well beaten: Use a mixer and beat eggs 5 to 10 minutes, until they are thick and lemon–colored.

To make egg whites stiffly beaten: Never add sugar to the egg whites before they are beaten. Beat the egg whites until they are frothy, or until soft peaks form—then slowly add the sugar. The expansion of the air in egg whites is the leavening in soufflés, macaroons, and angel food cakes.

Flour

All-Purpose Flour

This is the most frequently used flour and, unless otherwise noted, what I use in all the recipes in this cookbook. It is a blend of soft and hard wheats.

Self-Rising Flour

Baking powder and salt are added to basic flour, making it ideal for quick breads. It is not suitable for yeast breads. Do not add yeast to this flour.

Cake Flour

Softer and whiter than all-purpose flour, it's perfect for delicate cakes.

Whole Wheat, Bran, Rye, Buckwheat, Oatmeal, and Cornmeal

You don't need to sift these flours, just stir them, measure into measuring cups, and use as directed in recipe.

Sifting Flour

If you live in an area where the humidity is high, it is necessary to sift flour to remove the lumps. You can use a strainer if you prefer.

Occasionally, tiny bugs like to live and die in flour. Sifting will sort them out and prevent them from appearing as tiny dots in your baked goods.

Leavenings

Yeast, baking powder, and baking soda are leavenings. When a batter containing one of these ingredients is heated, gas, air, or steam expands—making the finished product lighter in grain and texture.

Yeast

Yeast is a tiny plant that produces carbon dioxide when combined with sugar and when temperatures and moisture are right for its growth. It comes in compressed and powdered forms and should be used according to package directions.

Baking Powder

Baking powder releases a small amount of gas when mixed with liquid and heated. Recipes in this book are based on double-acting baking powder.

Baking Soda

When mixed with a liquid such as buttermilk, sour milk, vinegar, molasses, or lemon juice, baking soda gives off a gas that helps baked goods rise. You can replace baking powder by mixing ¼ teaspoon baking soda with ½ cup of sour milk.

Sugar

Granulated Sugar

Made from beets or cane, it is now available organically as well as processed. Granulated sugar is the sugar used in all of the recipes in this cookbook unless I specify powdered, extra-fine, or brown sugar.

Brown Sugar

Brown sugar is less refined than granulated sugar, dark brown sugar contains more molasses than light brown sugar and has a more intense flavor.

Powdered Sugar

Powdered sugar is granulated sugar that has been crushed to an extreme fineness and mixed with a small amount of corn starch. Also called confectioners' sugar, this is often used in frostings. It has been my experience in baking cookies that the finer the sugar, the less the cookie expands.

Extra-Fine Sugar

Granulated sugar that has been crushed to a fine texture is not the same as powdered sugar, and is sometimes difficult to find on grocery shelves. I used it exclusively at the bakery because it gives cakes a finer texture and it melts more quickly and completely than granulated sugar. If you can't find extra-fine sugar, place a cup of granulated in your food processor with a metal blade and process for 30 seconds.

Milk

Lowfat Milk

Most of the butterfat (98 percent) has been removed from whole milk.

Nonfat or Skim Milk

Contains less than 0.5 percent butterfat.

Homogenized Milk

Has been treated so that the cream does not separate from the milk. When I was a child, milkmen left the milk in a special storage compartment outside the kitchen. It was a wonderful sight to see the cream that had frozen and stood as a cap outside the glass bottle.

Evaporated Milk

Over 50 percent of the water has been removed from whole milk. Undiluted, it may be used in place of cream. When chilled and ice crystals form, it can be whipped.

Sweetened Condensed Milk

A thick blend of evaporated whole milk and sugar. You cannot substitute regular evaporated milk in its place. Making it yourself will save you a great deal of money. This actually gets thicker and better with time.

4 cups instant powdered milk
1 cup very hot water
2 cups sugar
4 tablespoons butter, melted

Mix all the ingredients in a mixer or a blender. Store in the refrigerator in a jar with a tightly fitting lid.

Makes 2 cups

Hint: It can be stored indefinitely in your refrigerator. Be sure to mark the jar so it doesn't turn into mystery mix.

Butter

Butter is commonly available in quarter-pound sticks, which are marked off in tablespoon increments. For the recipes in this cookbook, 1 stick of butter equals 8 tablespoons.

Clarified Butter

Gourmet chefs clarify butter because commercially produced butter has lots of excess water or whey. When this whey is removed from butter by clarification, it is possible to heat the butter to high temperatures without having it smoke and burn.

Although none of the recipes in this book specifically calls for clarified butter, the finished product is a little richer when you use clarified butter.

To clarify butter, place the butter in the top of a double boiler over boiling water. The butter will melt and the milky sediment will separate from the melted butter. Pour off the clear fat—this is the clarified butter—and discard the whey.

Baking Supplies

For mail order information on candy–and cake-making supplies, contact:
Jeannie Lutz
Sugar & Spice
3200 Balboa
San Francisco, CA 94121
Tel: 415/387-1722; Fax: 415/387-7133

Her store is crammed with everything you could ever need and she is very informative, knowledgeable, and cooperative.

Notes on Chocolate

$\mathcal{C}$hocolate is made from the bean of the cocoa tree grown in tropical areas near the equator. The beans are dried, roasted, and ground into a thick paste made smooth and mellow by an intense rolling process. The flavor of the chocolate depends on the roasting of the beans and the area where they are grown.

Chocolate is composed of cocoa solids and cocoa butter, the purest form of vegetable fat available. The proportions of these ingredients and the amount of sugar, flavoring, and milk solids determine the type of chocolate produced. The finest chocolate contains as much as 50 percent cocoa butter. Less expensive chocolate contains vegetable oils or shortening to replace expensive cocoa butter that has been removed from the powdered cocoa.

Chocolate Flavors

Bittersweet or Semisweet Chocolate

These chocolates contain enough sugar to make them good enough to eat alone and are my personal favorites for baking and coating.

Unsweetened or Baking Chocolate

Unsweetened or baking chocolate contains no sugar. It is used in only in a few recipes here. It is too bitter to eat alone.

White Chocolate

The names *white chocolate* or *summer chocolate* are really misnomers, as this "chocolate" contains no cocoa liquor. In inexpensive white chocolate the cocoa butter is replaced by coconut oil, palm oil, or shortening. White chocolate burns easily; melt it in the top of a double boiler.

Milk Chocolate

Dried or condensed milk replaces some of the cocoa solids in this chocolate, resulting in a sweeter flavor. It is sensitive to heat, difficult to work with, and requires patience and practice. I seldom use it for baking.

I have not had much success melting milk chocolate in a microwave; instead, I use the top of a double boiler over hot, but not boiling, water.

Cocoa Powder

Unsweetened pure chocolate from which most of the cocoa butter has been removed becomes *cocoa powder*. Dutch-processed or alkalized cocoa is easiest to work with because of its mild flavor and ease in dissolving.

Sweetened cocoa is also called *powdered chocolate* and usually contains powdered milk; this type of powder is frequently used for drinks but is not generally used in baking. I like to roll uncoated candies in sweetened cocoa powder.

Chocolate Coating

Also known as *dipping chocolate* or *couveture*, chocolate coating contains a high percentage of cocoa butter and is available in bittersweet, white, and milk chocolate flavors.

Chocolate coating melts easily and smoothly and produces high-gloss decorations. I have been very successful at melting the semisweet chocolate in a microwave. I use the top of a double boiler over hot, but not boiling, water to melt milk chocolate and white chocolate.

Chocolate A'peels

Chocolate A'peels, made by the Guittard Chocolate Company, are chocolate wafers available in candy supply stores. Imitation chocolate, A'peels contain no cocoa butter, are less creamy than real chocolate, are easy to work with, and are available in white, milk, and dark chocolate wafers packed in 1-pound bags. The wafers are easily melted in a microwave. Unless you are a real gourmet and have a highly sensitive palate, you may not realize that this is imitation chocolate.

If you can't find A'peels, try using imitation chocolate chips. I found something called *chocolate bark* at the supermarket packed in 1-ounce squares in 2-pound bags, which worked fine.

Imitation chocolate is also sensitive to moisture, so keep it dry!

Handling Chocolate

Chopping Chocolate

Never try to chop warm chocolate. I freeze my chocolate block, wrap it in heavy plastic, set it on concrete, and use a hammer to break it into small pieces. A chef's knife or ice-carving pick work well, too.

Melting Chocolate

Bittersweet, semisweet, and unsweetened chocolate can be melted in a microwave. If you are melting 8 ounces or less, use an 8-cup Pyrex measuring cup. The handle will make handling the melted chocolate easier.

Chop the chocolate and heat on high for 1 minute at a time. Chocolate burns easily. Check it as often as every 30 seconds. When it just starts to melt, stir the chocolate using a wooden spoon. *Do not overheat!*

I have not had much success melting milk chocolate or white chocolate in a microwave. Instead, I place it in the top of a double boiler over hot, but not boiling, water.

As you melt chocolate, do not cover it. If chocolate comes into contact with a small amount of water, such as condensation from a lid, it will seize and turn into a thick, grainy mass. To undo a seizure, try adding a tablespoon of vegetable oil. Continue to stir it gently over low heat until the mass returns to a smooth consistency.

Also be aware that adding ingredients to chocolate as it melts may cause it to seize. To prevent this, add ingredients at the same temperature as your chocolate; never add a liquid that is much hotter or colder. And, of course, there is nothing sadder than burning chocolate. There is no remedy once it is scorched.

Tempering Chocolate

Tempering restores chocolate that has become streaked with white to its original state. Technically, you are breaking down the chocolate crystals. Tempering takes patience and practice and is best done on couveture or chocolate coating that has a high cocoa butter content.

Melt the chocolate in the top of a double boiler and stir with a wooden spoon until it is very smooth and has reached a temperature of 115° on a candy thermometer. Set the bowl of melted chocolate on a dry towel and let it cool to 80°. Reheat the chocolate until it reaches 90°. Now it's ready to use. If you are working with a great quantity of dipping chocolate, use a heating pad or an electric cooking pot set on low to keep chocolate at a consistent temperature.

Storing Chocolate

The ideal place to store chocolate should be cool and dry and between 65° and 70°. I have not had much luck storing chocolate in the refrigerator because it is too humid; however, I have stored chocolate in the freezer for several years at a time.

If your chocolate turns whitish, it is out of temper. It will still taste good and can be successfully returned to its original state by retempering. See the instructions for tempering chocolate earlier in this chapter.

Chocolate Decorations

Use chocolate to decorate the sides of cakes and to impress everyone— and yourself!

Cut a strip of parchment paper the width and height of your cake. Brush or spread cooled, melted chocolate over the paper and immediately wrap it around the side of your cake, paper side out. Refrigerate until set, about an hour. Peel off the paper, and voilà! Elegance!

Chocolate Curls

For an impressive decoration, take a block of chocolate at room temperature, hold at an angle, and shave away curls of chocolate using a vegetable peeler. Work over a piece of paper then refrigerate the curls until you use them.

Chocolate Rounds, Squares, or Triangles

You will need patience, practice, and parchment paper for these decorations. Spread melted, cooled chocolate on paper. Let the chocolate harden and cut it into shapes with a sharp knife. If the chocolate cracks, use the crumbs as decorations. They're still impressive.

Piping Chocolate Decorations

Are you ready to be a big-time show-off? Draw decorative designs on parchment paper. Fill a clean plastic mustard or ketchup bottle with melted, cooled chocolate. Squeeze the chocolate onto the paper in the shape of the designs. When set, remove the decorations from the paper and use to trim cakes and tortes.

Chocolate Clay

You need very cold hands and patience to mold roses by hand or create your own sculptural pieces. This clay works best if refrigerated overnight.

10 ounces bittersweet or semisweet chocolate, melted and cooled
⅓ cup white corn syrup

Mix the melted chocolate and corn syrup together. Cover and store overnight in the refrigerator. Next day, allow it to come to room temperature before working it into shapes.

Hint: If you want to learn techniques for molding, decorating, and designing with chocolate, read Elaine Gonzales's book *Chocolate Artistry* (Contemporary Press). Elaine is a charming lady with great knowledge and skill, and her book is filled with instructional photographs.

Elaine taught me how to make chocolate roses. Create small rounds of chocolate clay and press individual balls into petal shapes. Then press the petals together to make a rose.

At Chocoholics Bakery we decorated our cakes with chocolate roses, using chocolate frosting. They were beautiful and delicious. You can also make chocolate roses using a decorating tube and the instructions in Elaine's book as well as the Wilton Company instructions.

Chocolate Bowl

Fill these chocolate bowls with your favorite filling for an elegant dessert.

1 pound chocolate A'peels or imitation chocolate

Melt the chocolate, then allow it to cool to 90°. Inflate a small balloon and dip the bottom of the balloon in the chocolate. Turn the balloon until a bowl shape is formed. Set the chocolate-dipped balloon on wax paper until it is completely dry and hardened.

Deflate the balloon and peel it away from the bowl.

After you have some experience, mix the chocolate colors, dip the balloon in one color, let it set, then dip in another color. Voilà, you are an artist!

Chocolate Dessert Cups

Make traditional shapes using muffin cups or coat the interiors of small paper bags with chocolate to create unique serving containers.

4 ounces semisweet or milk chocolate
4 muffin cups

Heat the chocolate until it is almost melted. Remove from heat and stir until the chocolate is completely melted. Use a small brush to coat the insides of the muffin cups. Recoat several times until the desired thickness is reached. Peel away the paper cups and fill them with ice cream, whipped cream, mousse, or whatever seems delicious!

Chocolate Coating

Use this coating to dip truffles, candies, fruits, nuts, cookies, or anything else you might want to coat in chocolate.

1 pound semisweet chocolate, chopped into small pieces
1 tablespoon vegetable oil*

Use a microwave or the top of a double boiler to melt the chocolate and oil to 85° on a candy thermometer. Use a toothpick or a fondue fork to handle the candy you wish to coat. Dip the candy into the chocolate. Reheat the chocolate if it hardens.

Set the dipped candies on wax paper and allow to dry at room temperature. Be adventurous. Decorate these fabulous goodies anyway you like. This could start a whole new career for you; it did for me!

Hint: *If you use Chocolate A'peels, eliminate the vegetable oil.

Chocolate-Dipped Nuts & Fruits

You can use any fruit or nut you like: fresh strawberries, sliced peaches, bananas, cherries, fresh raspberries, dried fruits, or nuts.

Melt the chocolate and dip the fruits and/or nuts. Place on waxed paper to dry. Do not refrigerate after dipping or the chocolate will become sticky (referred to by candymakers as *blooming*).

Hint: Mix any remaining chocolate crumbs with nuts and raisins, and drop by spoonfuls onto waxed paper to create chocolate clusters.

Chocolate-Dipped Cookies

Oreos and filled cookies are the best for dipping. Dip one side of the cookie in chocolate and place it on wax paper to dry or drop the whole cookie into melted chocolate and use a fondue fork to lift it out.

Fancy Touches

If you want your cookies (or fruit) picture-perfect, dip one side in dark or milk chocolate and place on wax paper to dry. Once the chocolate is set, dip the other side of the fruit or cookie into melted white chocolate.

Fancier still? Fill a clean plastic squeeze bottle with colored imitation chocolate, melted and cooled, and drizzle different colors over the chocolate-coated fruits, nuts, or cookies.

HEAVENLY CAKES

$\mathcal{O}$kay, the truth is out. I didn't start baking until I was 52 years old. I gained a real education when the dessert parlor hit a financial skid and I realized we needed to do something different, something that had never been done before in Humboldt County.

I couldn't find anyone whose products were good enough to sell at our parlor, so everyday for a year I tried a new cake or cheesecake or pie recipe and served it at the parlor at night. People bought it and ate it and loved it.

I also experimented with packaged cake mixes. In fact, because many bakeries face financial difficulties (buying butter, eggs, flour, chocolate, and other expensive ingredients really adds up!) and bakers can be a cantankerous bunch (late nights out and early work hours often clash), most bakeries rely on mixes of some sort. To help you simplify your life, this chapter provides several recipes for cakes made with mix!

Hints for Perfect Cakes

- Butter your cake pans with butter or spray them with a light coating of nonstick spray. Sprinkle flour into each pan and shake it until it is coated. Tap out the excess flour.
- Invest in a sugar shaker with a handle. Buy one with holes larger than a salt shaker. Fill the shaker with flour and this will make the messy job of "dust lightly with flour" simple. Be sure to label the shaker so you can identify it in the future!
- Fill your pans no more than two-thirds full of batter and make sure the batter is spread all the way into the sides and corners of the baking pan.

- When the cake is baked it should shrink slightly from the sides of the pan. Invest in a small cake tester (they only cost about $1), which resembles a wire with a plastic button on the end. A tester inserted into the center of the cake will come out clean when the cake is done. This is the most accurate way of knowing if your cake is thoroughly baked.
- I have discovered that the best way to keep a cake from sinking or falling is to place the hot cake pan directly onto a tea towel that has been soaked in water and wrung out. The cake pan will make a hissing sound, but for some miraculous reason the cake will cool perfectly and come out almost as high as it was when it was taken out of the oven.
- If you need a cake rack, try using the rack from your oven. The wires are a little wide but it works if the cake is cool.
- Freeze the cake layers for at least 1 hour before frosting them. Most cake layers can be covered with foil or clear plastic wrap and stored for weeks and even months before using them. I always keep a few cake layers in the freezer for quick cakes.
- Before you frost cake layers, brush off the crumbs.
- Spray or brush simple syrup (recipe follows) on the layers to ensure that your cake is moist and will keep for at least a week.
- See hints on decorating cakes in the Notes on Chocolate chapter if you are new at cake making.

Have a wonderful time baking these recipes. Remember that if a cake should fail for any reason, don't discard it. Make trifle.

Simple Syrup

Makes
2 cups

The secret to a moist, long-lasting cake can now be told. You can purchase simple syrup in a bar or restaurant supply store or make it yourself. It keeps for a long time.

1 cup sugar
1 cup white corn syrup or dextrose
1 cup water

Combine all the ingredients in a saucepan and bring to a full boil. Allow it to cool before using. Brush a liberal amount (about 2 tablespoons) of simple syrup on each cake layer, or, to make the job even easier, fill a spray bottle with simple syrup and spritz the layers.

Hint: If you are in a hurry, boil together 1 cup sugar and 1 cup water and use it as soon as it is cool. This mixture will not keep, but it will form beautiful crystals.

Magic Cake Mix

Serves
12 to 18

Here's a totally fail-proof cake recipe with variations on a theme. I prefer to use Duncan Hines cake mix because it's sifted a jillion times.

1 (18.25-ounce) box cake mix, any flavor
1 (3.4-ounce) box vanilla instant pudding
4 eggs
1 cup water
½ cup vegetable or canola oil

Preheat oven to 350°. Butter two 8-inch cake pans and dust them lightly with flour.

Combine all ingredients. Mix for 30 seconds on low speed, then mix for 2 minutes on medium speed. Pour batter into the prepared cake pans.

Bake 20 to 25 minutes, or until a cake tester inserted into the center of the cake comes out clean. Cool the layers for 15 minutes then remove from pans. Freeze the layers 1 hour. Brush or spray them liberally with simple syrup before frosting.

Hint: If you want to make a really big cake, use three 10-inch cake pans and two boxes of cake mix.

Apple Chunk Cake

Serves
12 to 18

This is an absolutely wonderful cake and one of my personal favorites despite the fact that it is not chocolate. It is a very moist cake, stays fresh for a week, and doesn't require frosting. I prefer using crisp, tart apples.

1½ cups vegetable or canola oil
2 cups sugar
3 large eggs
3 cups flour
Pinch of salt
1 teaspoon baking soda

6 Granny Smith apples, peeled, cored, and cut into cubes
2 cups chopped pecans
1 tablespoon vanilla or maple extract

Preheat oven to 350°. Spray a Bundt pan with nonstick spray and dust lightly with flour.

Combine oil and sugar and beat until thick. Add eggs, one at a time, and beat until smooth. Add flour, salt, and baking soda. Mix in apples, pecans, and vanilla or maple extract. Pour batter into the prepared pan and spread evenly.

Bake cake 1 hour, or until cake tests done. Remove the layers from the oven and allow them to cool. If you choose to decorate this cake, I suggest using the following glaze.

Easy Glaze

When the cake is cooled, place a can of prepared lemon or vanilla frosting in the microwave for 45 seconds. Stir the frosting and drizzle it over the cake then decorate with pecan halves.

Hint: This is a very dense cake. Make sure the center of the cake is fully baked before removing it from the oven.

Fresh Raspberry Cream Cake

Serves
12 to 18

Almost everyone loves the flavor of raspberries. If you can find a fine raspberry flavoring, use it. Otherwise use fresh raspberries or frozen raspberries that have been defrosted and drained through a strainer.

1 (18.25-ounce) box white cake mix
1 (3.4-ounce) box instant pudding
4 egg whites
1 cup water
⅓ cup vegetable or canola oil
1 tablespoon raspberry flavoring, or 2 cups fresh or frozen raspberries
Simple syrup
2 cups whipping cream
¼ cup powdered sugar

If you are using frozen raspberries, save the drained juice and add enough water to make 1 cup. Your cake will be pink and pretty.

Preheat oven to 350°. Butter two 8-inch cake pans and dust lightly with flour.

Combine cake mix, pudding, egg whites, water, oil, and raspberry flavoring and mix until smooth. Pour the batter into the prepared cake pans and bake 20 to 25 minutes, or until the cake tests done.

Remove the cakes from the oven and cool the layers by placing them on a slightly dampened tea towel. (This will prevent the layers from sinking.) When the layers are cooled, remove them from the pans and freeze them for 1 hour after you have sprayed or brushed the layers with simple syrup.

Whip cream until very frothy. Add powdered sugar and beat until stiff. Cover the sides and top of the cake with whipped cream and decorate with fresh raspberries. Keep cake refrigerated until served.

Hint: You can replace the raspberries with almost any fresh berry: blackberries, boysenberries, blueberries, or with canned cherries in syrup or peaches or pears that have been drained of their juice.

Moist and Creamy Banana Cake

**Serves
12 to 18**

A very old cake recipe, this was given to me when my daughter was born and is her very favorite cake. It's moist and delicious.

1¾ cups sugar
1 stick butter, at room temperature
3 large eggs
4 very ripe bananas
2½ cups flour
1 tablespoon baking soda
Pinch of salt
⅔ cup buttermilk
½ cup chopped nuts (optional)
¼ cup chopped dates or raisins (optional)

Preheat oven to 350°. Butter two 8-inch cake pans and dust lightly with flour.

Cream together butter and sugar. Add eggs and bananas and mix. In a separate bowl, blend flour, baking soda, and salt. Add dry ingredients and buttermilk alternately to the egg-banana mixture. Beat until smooth. Add the nuts, raisins, and dates if desired.

Bake 30 minutes, or until the cake tests done. (This is a dense and heavy cake. Make sure it is thoroughly baked before removing it from the oven.) Remove the cake from oven and place on a slightly damp tea towel to cool (this will prevent the layers from sinking).

Allow the cake to cool. Dust the layers with powdered sugar or spread your favorite chocolate frosting between the layers and decorate the top and sides of the cake with Whipped Cream Frosting (page 82). This cake is very moist and doesn't need simple syrup. Mmmmm good!

Hint: This recipe also makes marvelous muffins and banana bread.

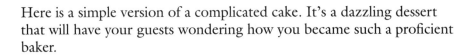 Black Forest Cake

Serves
12 to 18

Here is a simple version of a complicated cake. It's a dazzling dessert that will have your guests wondering how you became such a proficient baker.

2 frozen chocolate cake layers (use a mix or follow one of my chocolate cake recipes)
Simple syrup
1 (16-ounce) can of chocolate frosting
3 cups whipping cream
½ cup powdered sugar
1 can cherry pie filling, reserve juice
1 tablespoon unsweetened cocoa
1 tablespoon vanilla

Remove frozen cake layers from freezer. Split them in half horizontally and apply simple syrup to the layers while they are still frozen. Spread chocolate frosting generously on all the layers.

Whip the cream until frothy and slowly add powdered sugar. Continue beating until cream is stiff. Using ½ cup of the whipped cream, thicken the cherry juice from the canned filling. Spread some cherries on top of one frosted layer and cover with the cherry-flavored whipped cream. Top this with a half layer of frosted cake.

Add cocoa to another ½ cup of whipped cream. Spread cherries on top of the second frosted layer and spread the chocolate whipping cream on top.

Add vanilla to ½ cup whipping cream. Spread cherries on top of the third frosted layer and spread vanilla whipping cream over the cherries. Cover with the last half layer of cake. Press the layers together and freeze the entire cake for at least 1 hour.

Remove cake from freezer and frost the top with chocolate or use the remaining cherry pie filling. Frost the sides of the cake with the remaining 1½ cups whipped cream. Refrigerate cake until it is served.

Hint: This cake will not keep well in the refrigerator for more than 12 to 24 hours unless it has been frozen. If you prepare this cake several days in advance, keep it in your freezer, uncovered. Remove from freezer 12 to 24 hours before serving and store in the refrigerator.

Gingerbread Cake

Serves
12 to 18

It's not chocolate but it is a super cake and perfect to serve a big crowd at Halloween. Serve warm with whipped cream.

1 (16-ounce) jar applesauce
2 teaspoons baking soda
1 cup dark molasses
3 cups sifted flour
2 teaspoons salt
2 teaspoons powdered ginger
½ teaspoon ground cloves
4 eggs
1⅓ cups sugar
⅔ cup vegetable oil
1 (16-ounce) can vanilla frosting

Preheat oven to 325°. Spray a 10-inch tube pan or a Bundt pan with nonstick spray and dust lightly with flour.

Bring applesauce to boil in a large saucepan. Add baking soda and molasses. Set aside to cool.

Stir the flour and spices together.

Beat eggs until thick and lemon-colored. Beat in the sugar. Gradually beat in the oil. Add the applesauce mixture and the flour-spice mixture alternately.

Pour batter into the prepared pan and bake 1 hour and 15 minutes. Cool 15 minutes. Invert the cake onto a serving plate and dust it with powdered sugar or drizzle melted, canned vanilla frosting over the top. (A microwave works well for melting frosting.)

Serve warm or cold.

Caramel Crunch Cake

Serves
18

This cake is not low in calories, fat, or cholesterol. But, oh, it is mighty high in taste and fun. Bake it in a 9 x 13-inch baking dish so that you won't have to frost it, or you can bake in two 8-inch pans and frost it with whipped cream or dark chocolate. It is wonderful!

1 (18.25-ounce) box caramel flavor cake mix
1 (3.4-ounce) box butterscotch instant pudding
1 cup coffee or water
⅓ cup oil
4 large eggs
3 king-size (3.7-ounce) Baby Ruth candy bars, sliced into thin bits

Crunchy Topping

1 cup flaked coconut
1 cup chopped nuts
½ stick butter

Preheat oven to 350°. Butter a 9 x 13-inch pan and dust lightly with flour.

Use a mixer to combine the cake mix, pudding mix, coffee or water, oil, and eggs, and beat until smooth. Stir in the chopped candy bars. Pour batter into the prepared pan.

Prepare Crunchy Topping by stirring ingredients together and spread on the cake before putting it into the oven.

Bake cake 40 minutes, or until the cake tests done. Serve warm or cold.

Chocolate Variation

Reserve 1 cup of the batter and stir 4 ounces of chocolate sauce into the batter. Pour the chocolate mixture in a zigzag pattern over the cake. Run a table knife gently through the batter to form a marbleized pattern.

Rosie's Angel Food Cake

Serves
12 to 18

Rose Naftalan owned Rose's Bakery in Portland, Oregon. Her cakes were enormous. Although I did not see her cakes until I had been baking for several years, she became my inspiration. I never got to meet her in person, but I did have the honor of speaking to her on the phone and she gave me this recipe.

1½ cups cake flour
2 cups extra-fine sugar
2 cups (about 12) egg whites
2 teaspoons cream of tartar
Pinch of salt
1 teaspoon vanilla

Preheat oven to 350°. Use an ungreased angel food cake pan or a 10-inch tube pan.

Mix flour and ¼ cup of the sugar together and sift the combination five times. Use a strainer if you prefer. Set aside.

Beat egg whites until almost stiff. Add cream of tartar and salt and continue beating, adding the remaining sugar gradually.

When the eggs look shiny and stiff, carefully fold in the sifted flour and vanilla.

Pour batter into pan and place in the oven. Bake 10 minutes at 350°.

Reduce oven temperature to 325° and bake the cake 30 additional minutes at this heat. Reduce the oven temperature to 300° and bake cake until it tests done, about 1 hour. Remove cake from the oven and invert it to cool.

Remove cake from the pan when it is cool and frost—or leave it plain. This cake is low in calories and cholesterol free.

Chocolate Cashew Cake

Serves
12 to 18

If you love cashews and are a chocoholic, this cake is for you: a very dense, brownie-like cake with an incredible frosting. It's very intense so a tiny serving will satisfy.

½ cup semisweet chocolate chips
2½ ounces unsweetened chocolate
¾ stick butter
5 eggs
1 cup sugar
1 teaspoon vanilla
¾ cup flour
Pinch of salt
¾ teaspoon baking powder
3 tablespoons sour cream

Preheat oven to 325° and coat a 9-inch cake pan with butter. Dust lightly with flour. Use a sugar shaker filled with flour to make this easy.

Melt chocolate chips, unsweetened chocolate, and butter in the microwave. Stir until smooth.

Use a mixer to combine the eggs, sugar, and vanilla and beat 5 minutes, or until the volume of the eggs has doubled. Add the melted chocolate mixture and beat slightly.

Fold in the flour, salt, and baking powder by hand until thoroughly mixed. Pour batter into the prepared pan and bake 1 hour or until the cake tests done.

Remove cake from the oven and allow it to cool for 1 hour. Prepare the ganache to use for filling and frosting this cake.

Chocolate Ganache

3 cups unroasted cashews
3 tablespoons sugar
½ cup whipping cream
3 tablespoons sweet butter
2 cups semisweet chocolate chips, or 12 ounces fine semisweet
  chocolate

Preheat oven to 325°. Spread cashews on a cookie sheet and toast for 10 minutes, or until they are golden brown.

Remove nuts from oven and pour them onto another cookie sheet covered in paper towels to cool completely. Save 18 whole cashews to decorate the finished cake. Use a food processor with a metal blade to chop the nuts, ½ cup at a time, into small pieces.

Heat together sugar, whipping cream, and butter. Bring mixture to a boil and add chocolate chips. Stir until well mixed. Save 1 cup of this ganache. Mix the chopped cashews into the remaining ganache and keep at room temperature until needed.

Remove the cake from the refrigerator and slice the layer into three sections horizontally. Spread some ganache between the layers and on top of the cake. Press layers together and refrigerate until the ganache is firm.

Spread the remaining ganache on the sides of the cake. Hold the cake in one hand over a large bowl and press remaining chopped cashews into the frosting on the sides of the cake. Decorate the top of the cake with the whole cashews and refrigerate until served.

Hint: Use two boxes of brownie mix and bake the cake in a 9-inch springform pan. Cut the cooled layer into thirds, spread layers with ganache, and place the filled cake into the springform pan. Refrigerate cake 1 hour, then remove the springform by running a knife around the edges. Use remaining ganache to decorate the top and sides of the cake and press remaining chopped cashews into the side of the frosting. Fantastic!

Lemon Poppy Seed Pound Cake

Serves
12 to 16

I created this recipe especially for this cookbook. It is a moist, melt-in-your-mouth cake and as close to perfection as possible—foolproof comfort food.

2 tablespoons poppy seeds
¾ cup water
1 box lemon cake mix
1 small box lemon instant pudding
1 tablespoon lemon extract
¾ cup sour cream
⅓ cup vegetable or canola oil
3 eggs

Soak poppy seeds in ¾ cup water 1 hour.

Preheat oven to 350° and spray a Bundt pan with nonstick spray. Dust lightly with flour.

Combine all the ingredients, including poppy seeds, and beat until smooth, about 2 minutes. Pour into prepared pan and bake 40 minutes, or until cake tests done.

Remove cake from oven and place on a slightly damp dish towel until almost cool. This will prevent the cake from sinking. When it is completely cooled, invert the cake onto a cake platter. This is living!

Hint: Serve with Lemon Curd (page 78), whipped cream, or fresh fruit.

Chocolate Pound Cake

Serves
12 to 18

Follow the recipe for Lemon Poppy Seed Pound Cake and eliminate lemon cake mix, lemon extract, lemon pudding, and poppy seeds. Add 1 cup semisweet chocolate chips and 1 cup chopped nuts. Bake 50 minutes, or until cake tests done.

When cake is cool, microwave a can of chocolate frosting for 40 seconds. Stir the frosting and drizzle over the cake in an interesting pattern. Top with nut halves.

Hint: You can always change the flavor of this pound cake by using the same recipe and different flavors of cake mixes.

If you want a creamy center, pour ½ can of frosting in a circle in the center of the cake before baking.

Chocoholics Cake

Serves
18 to 24

Here is an absolutely foolproof way to make that famous three-layered, three-flavored chocolate cake that we used to serve in our bakery. You will have a total of six layers, so you can make two cakes or store three layers in the freezer until you are ready to decorate and serve another.

1 (18.25-ounce) box Swiss chocolate cake mix
1 (18.25-ounce) box devil's food cake mix
1 (18.25-ounce) box dark chocolate cake mix
12 eggs
3 cups water
1 cup vegetable or canola oil
3 (3.4-ounce) boxes instant pudding
Simple syrup
1 (16-ounce) can chocolate frosting

Preheat oven to 350°. Butter two 8- or 9-inch cake pans and dust lightly with flour. You will be baking one mix at a time (unless you have six cake pans available).

To prepare each box of mix: add 4 eggs, 1 cup water, ⅓ cup oil, and 1 box instant pudding. Mix on low for 1 minute. Beat on high for 2 minutes, or until well blended.

Pour batter into prepared pans and bake 20 to 25 minutes, or until the cake tests done. Cool and remove the layers from the pans.

Follow these steps with each box of mix until you have six layers, two of each flavor.

Freeze the baked and cooled layers at least 1 hour. Cut the rounded tops off the cake layers so that they are all level. Save the leftover cake for Rum Balls (page 195). Spray or brush simple syrup on each layer. Spread frosting between the layers.

Freeze the layer cake until it is firm enough to frost the top and sides. If you are going to write on the top of the cake, do that before applying the final decorations.

Hint: This cake is exquisite decorated with whipped cream and fresh flowers.

Honeycomb Crunch Cake

**Serves
12 to 18**

Lots of customers asked for this cake, which was a favorite at the long-gone Blum's Bakery in San Francisco. It is still available at the famous Madonna Inn in San Luis Obispo.

Use a prepared 9-inch sponge cake or angel food cake and cover it with sweet whipping cream and crushed honeycomb candy. Or bake your own layers following one of my recipes.

This cake doesn't keep well. You have to make it, refrigerate it, and eat it in a few hours. But oh, it is delicious!

Honeycomb Crunch

1 ¼ cups white corn syrup
1 ½ cups fine sugar
¼ cup strong coffee
3 teaspoons sifted baking soda

This topping can be made the day before. Stir the corn syrup, sugar, and coffee into a deep saucepan and bring to a boil.

Continue heating topping until it reaches 310° on a candy thermometer or until a small amount dropped into cold water breaks with a snap.

Remove mixture from heat. Get ready for excitement! Stir baking soda into the mixture until it thickens, foams, and pulls away from the pan. Don't overbeat. Pour batter onto an ungreased cookie sheet. Don't try to smooth the mixture onto the pan. Let it harden and cool completely.

Honeycomb Crunch Cake

1 (9-inch) frozen sponge cake or angel food cake
2 cups whipping cream
¼ cup powdered sugar
1 tablespoon vanilla

If you make your own, freeze the cake layers at least 1 hour. Cut already frozen cake into thirds horizontally. Crumble Honeycomb Crunch topping between sheets of wax paper.

Whip cream until frothy; slowly add powdered sugar and vanilla and whip the cream until stiff.

Spread the whipped cream between the layers and on top of the cake. Sprinkle crushed Honeycomb Crunch all over the top of the cake and press the candy into the sides of the cream-covered cake.

Refrigerate the cake until it is served.

Cranberry Cake

Serve this delicious cake on Thanksgiving or Christmas to rave reviews. I live within a few hours' drive of the cranberry bogs in Oregon. At harvest time the fields are flooded and the cranberries float to the surface of the water, turning the acreage into a beautiful burgundy-colored surface. I came home from such a trip and made this cake.

Cranberry Cake

1 (18.25-ounce) box French vanilla cake mix
4 egg whites
1 (3.4-ounce) box French vanilla instant pudding
½ cup water
½ cup sour cream
2 cups fresh cranberries, or dried cranberries reconstituted in hot water
Simple syrup

Preheat oven to 350°. Spray two 8-inch cake pans with vegetable spray and dust lightly with flour.

Mix all ingredients except cranberries together until well blended. Stir in cranberries by hand. Pour batter into the prepared pans and bake 20 to 25 minutes, or until the cakes test done.

Remove pans from the oven and place them on a slightly damp tea towel to cool; this prevents the layers from sinking. Remove layers from the pans when they are completely cooled and freeze them for 1 hour.

Remove layers from the freezer and spray or brush liberally with simple syrup.

Cranberry Frosting

2 cups whipping cream
¼ cup powdered sugar
1 tablespoon lemon juice
1 (8-ounce) can cranberry sauce

Whip the cream until frothy; add sugar and lemon juice. Beat until stiff. Mash cranberry sauce with a fork and fold into the whipped cream.

Decorate the top and sides and between the layers with this frosting. Refrigerate cake until served.

Hint: You can eliminate cranberry sauce from the frosting and use unflavored whipped cream. If you do, add an extra 1/4 cup powdered sugar to the whipped cream. Decorate the cake with holly leaves and cranberries.

Orange Chiffon Cake

Serves
12 to 18

A light, airy dessert—and low-calorie when the 10-inch springform tube pan you use is grease-free.

8 eggs, separated
1⅓ cups sugar
1 teaspoon grated orange peel
½ cup orange juice
1 cup sifted cake flour

Preheat oven to 325°. Beat the egg yolks and half of the sugar (⅔ cup) until thick and lemon-colored. Add orange juice and orange peel to the egg mixture alternately with the cake flour.

Beat egg whites until frothy; slowly add the other ⅔ cup sugar and continue beating until stiff. Gently fold the beaten whites into the batter using the side of your hand.

Bake in an ungreased tube pan 1 hour, 10 minutes. Invert and cool.

Hint: Frost with whipped cream or a microwaved can of orange frosting and drizzle the warm frosting over the cake. Decorate the cake with orange blossoms.

*R*ed Velvet Cake

Serves
12 to 18

This dramatic cake is moist and delicious.

1 stick butter at room temperature
1½ cups sugar
2 large eggs
2 tablespoons red food coloring
2 tablespoons water
2 tablespoons unsweetened cocoa
2 cups flour
1 cup buttermilk
1 teaspoon vanilla
1 tablespoon vinegar
1 teaspoon baking soda

Preheat oven to 350°. Butter two 8-inch cake pans and dust lightly with flour.

Cream together butter and sugar and beat until fluffy. Add eggs, food coloring, and water.

Add cocoa and flour alternately with buttermilk and beat until smooth. Add vanilla, vinegar, and baking soda last and just stir them into the batter.

Pour batter into the prepared pans and bake 30 minutes, or until the cake tests done.

Cool cake in pans 15 minutes. Remove the layers from the pans and continue to cool the layers.

Frost the cake with Chocolate Mousse Frosting (page 73).

Hint: The Food and Drug Administration has ordered food coloring manufacturers to remove the artificial ingredient that made red food coloring *really* red, so this may not be the cake you remember as a child.

German Chocolate Cake

Serves
18

Whether you choose to make the traditional or easy version of this cake, you'll find that the Coconut Pecan Frosting makes both versions irresistible.

1 (4-ounce) box Baker's German sweet chocolate
½ cup boiling water
1 cup butter
2 cups sugar
4 egg yolks
1 tablespoon vanilla
2 ½ cups sifted cake flour
1 teaspoon baking soda
Pinch of salt
1 cup buttermilk
4 egg whites, stiffly beaten

Preheat oven to 350°. Butter *three* 8-inch cake pans and dust lightly with flour.

Melt chocolate in boiling water. Cool.

Cream butter and sugar until light and fluffy. Add egg yolks, one at a time, beating after each addition. Add vanilla and melted chocolate. Mix well. Add dry ingredients alternately with buttermilk and beat until smooth.

Fold in the beaten egg whites carefully until mixture is blended. Pour batter into the prepared cake pans and bake 30 to 40 minutes, or until the layers test done. Cool the layers and freeze 1 hour before frosting them with Coconut Pecan Frosting (page 79).

Easy German Chocolate Cake

Prepare and bake a box of Swiss chocolate cake mix according to the Magic Cake Mix recipe (page 20).

Freeze the layers 1 hour.

Split the layers and fill them, then frost the top of the cake with Coconut Pecan Frosting (page 79). Frost the sides of the cake with the chocolate frosting of your choice and decorate the top of the cake with pecan halves.

Hint: No need to use simple syrup on the German Chocolate Cake layers because the frosting is very moist and will seep through the cake layers.

Butter Pecan Cake

It's hard to believe, but not everyone loves chocolate. Substitute yellow cake mixes for the Swiss chocolate mixes in the German Chocolate Cake recipe. Proceed with instructions. The result is a mouth-watering yellow cake with fabulous Coconut Pecan Frosting (page 79) seeping through the layers.

Oatmeal Cake

Serves
12

This old-fashioned cake recipe has been updated to make it simple to prepare. The frosting is broiled right on top of the cake. You can use a can of prepared frosting or follow the Coconut Pecan Frosting recipe on page 79.

1 stick butter, at room temperature
1 cup sugar
1 cup brown sugar, tightly packed
1 cup oatmeal
½ cup boiling water
2 tablespoons molasses
2 eggs
1½ cups flour
1 teaspoon baking soda
1 teaspoon cinnamon

Preheat oven to 350°. Butter an 8-inch square cake pan and lightly dust it with flour.

Use a mixer to cream together the butter and sugars until light and fluffy. Stir oatmeal into boiling water. Add the molasses, eggs, and oatmeal-water mixture to butter-sugar mixture. Gradually add dry ingredients and beat until well blended.

Spread batter into the prepared pan and bake 50 minutes, or until cake tests done.

Remove cake from the oven and allow to cool for 10 minutes. Spread frosting on top and place the cake six inches under the broiler until the top is lightly browned.

Chocolate Prune Cake

Serves
18

Dense, dark, and delicious, this cake is reminiscent of gingerbread.
Eliminate the spices and you still have a fantastic cake. Thanks, Lolita.

1½ cups sugar
1 cup oil
2 eggs
1 cup sour milk or buttermilk
2 cups flour
1 teaspoon baking powder
1 teaspoon baking soda
1 teaspoon salt
3 tablespoons cocoa
1 cup cooked, chopped prunes, or 1 jar (8 ounces) junior baby prunes
½ teaspoon *each* cloves and allspice (optional)
1 teaspoon cinnamon

Preheat oven to 350°. Butter a 9 x 13-inch pan or two 8-inch cake
pans. Dust lightly with flour.

Cream sugar and oil together and add remaining ingredients. Mix
until well blended. Pour into prepared pan and bake until cake tests
done, 40 to 50 minutes.

Dust the cooled cake with powdered sugar or frost it with Mocha
Buttercream Frosting (page 74).

Almost Solid Fruit and Nut Fruitcake

Serves 24 to 36

This is an adaptation of a fruitcake that was a winner in a *Sunset* magazine contest twenty years ago. It is almost solid fruit and nuts and contains very little batter. It's expensive to make but incredibly delicious.

1 cup dark raisins
1 cup golden raisins
1½ cups pitted prunes
1½ cups pitted dates
1½ cups dried figs
1½ cups dried apricots
1 cup whole brazil nuts
1 cup macadamia nuts
1 cup pecans

1 cup cashews
1 cup flour
4 eggs
3 tablespoons apple juice, rum, or brandy
Pinch of salt
1 tablespoon vanilla
½ cup sugar
1 cup dark corn syrup

Preheat oven to 300°. Combine all the fruits and nuts in a large bowl. Sprinkle ½ cup of the flour over the fruits and nuts and mix with your hands until coated with flour.

Lightly grease the sides and bottom of three loaf pans.

Beat eggs until thick and add apple juice, brandy, or rum, salt, vanilla, sugar, and the remaining ½ cup flour. Beat until well blended. Add the corn syrup and mix the batter with the fruit and nuts until the fruit and nuts are completely coated. I find it's easiest to mix everything together with your hands.

Scoop batter into the prepared pans and press down with your fingertips to make sure that the batter is evenly distributed in the pans.

Bake 1 hour or until the cake tests done. Place the loaf pans on a cookie sheet covered with foil to make handling the pans easier.

Remove cakes from oven and allow them to cool in the pans. When cakes are completely cooled, remove from pans.

This is an intense fruitcake—cut thin slices when serving.

Hint: These make marvelous gifts. Wrap the individual cakes in colored cellophane and tie with a pretty bow and some tiny paper flowers.

Black Russian Cake

Serves
12

An easy recipe using your Bundt pan. The cake is moist and rich and no one will suspect you used a mix—but they will wonder where you got such dark cocoa.

1 (18.25-ounce) box dark chocolate cake mix
⅓ cup vegetable or canola oil
4 eggs
1 (3.4-ounce) box chocolate instant pudding
½ cup very strong coffee
½ cup Kahlua
½ cup sour cream

Preheat oven to 350°. Spray a Bundt pan with nonstick spray and dust lightly with flour.

Combine all the ingredients and beat until smooth. Pour batter into pan.

Bake for 40 to 50 minutes, or until cake tests done.

Remove cake from oven and cool. Invert onto a serving plate. Punch holes in the cake and pour on topping.

Topping

1 cup powdered sugar
2 tablespoons very strong coffee
4 tablespoons Kahlua

Combine ingredients and pour through holes over the cake.

Chocolate Cream Cake

Serves
16

This cake is made without flour. I had lots of requests for it at Choco-holics Bakery from people who were allergic to flour. The icing is half of the batter and everyone who loves chocolate flips for this cake.

½ cup sugar
½ stick sweet butter, at room temperature
4 ounces semisweet chocolate, melted and cooled
8 eggs, separated
16 long-stemmed cherries

Preheat oven to 350°. Butter and flour an 8-inch square cake pan.

Using a mixer, cream the sugar and butter together until light and fluffy. Stir in the melted and cooled chocolate. Add egg yolks one at a time and mix well after each egg is added.

Beat the egg whites until very stiff. Carefully fold the chocolate mixture into the egg whites.

Pour half of the batter into the prepared pan. Cover and refrigerate the remaining batter. Reduce oven temperature to 300° immediately after you put the cake into the oven. Bake 45 minutes, or until the cake tests done.

Remove the cake from the oven and cool completely. Spread the remaining batter on top of the cake as a frosting and refrigerate over-night. Cut the cake into sixteen slices and decorate the top of each piece with a long-stemmed cherry.

Ice Cream Cake

Serves
12 to 18

Ice cream cake is easy to prepare and elegant to serve. It seems to please everyone. Use cake layers that have been stored in your freezer, or bake a box of cake mix—any flavor you prefer—and freeze layers until they are firm enough to be cut in half horizontally.

2 layers of cake, frozen and split in half
Simple syrup
2 (16-ounce) cans frosting
1 pint vanilla (or any flavor) ice cream
1 pint chocolate (or any flavor) ice cream
2 cups whipping cream
½ cup powdered sugar
1 tablespoon vanilla (or any flavoring)

Remove two cake layers from the freezer. Cut each layer in half horizontally. Spray or brush each layer generously with simple syrup and spread your favorite flavor of frosting over the tops of the layers.

Spread 1 pint slightly softened ice cream to fill between layers. Press down on each layer after it has been filled. Freeze the filled layers.

Whip cream until frothy. Add powdered sugar and vanilla (or your favorite) flavoring. Spread whipped cream over the top and sides of the ice cream-filled cake. Remove cake from freezer 30 minutes before serving.

Coffee Cake with Fruit and Streusel

Serves
12 to 18

This is similar to a fruit cobbler but with a streusel topping. Streusel is a combination of butter, sugar, and flour strewn on the tops of luscious coffee cakes served in elegant bakeries. You can keep it for a long time in an airtight can and sprinkle it on the top of muffins, coffee cakes, or cobblers.

Coffee Cake

½ stick butter, at room temperature
½ cup sugar
2 large eggs
1 teaspoon vanilla
¾ cup flour
⅓ cup cornstarch
4 tablespoons milk

Fruit Filling

4 tart apples, peeled, cored, seeded, and cut into thin wedges, or 6 ripe peaches, cored and sliced, or whatever fruit you prefer

Streusel

1 cup flour
⅓ cup sugar
1 teaspoon cinnamon
½ stick butter at room temperature

Work all streusel ingredients together using your fingers until crumbs are formed. Set aside.

Preheat oven to 350°. Butter and flour a 9 x 13-inch baking dish.

Prepare coffee cake. Cream together the butter and sugar. Beat in the eggs and vanilla. Add flour and cornstarch to the egg mixture and add enough milk to make the batter smooth. The batter should be thick. Pour batter into the prepared pan and smooth it evenly over the bottom of the pan.

Arrange the fruit filling in an overlapping pattern over the top of the batter, leaving a border of about ½ inch on the sides of the cake.

Sprinkle the streusel over the top.

Bake 30 to 40 minutes, or until cooked in the center. Serve warm right out of the pan.

Deep Chip Cake

**Serves
12 to 18**

This cake was my buddy Bill's idea and it was very popular at the bakery. The following is the easy way to prepare this cake.

1 (18.25-ounce) box dark chocolate cake mix
1 (3.4-ounce) box chocolate instant pudding
4 eggs
⅓ cup vegetable or canola oil
¾ cup sour cream
¾ cup water
2½ cups semisweet chocolate chips
Simple syrup
1 (16-ounce) can dark chocolate frosting

Preheat oven to 350°. Spray two 8-inch cake pans with vegetable spray and dust lightly with flour.

Mix together all ingredients except chocolate chips, simple syrup, and frosting. Blend until smooth. Add 2 cups chocolate chips.

Bake 25 to 30 minutes, or until the cake tests done. Remove the layers from the oven and cool.

Freeze the layers 1 hour, or until they are easy to handle. Brush or spray simple syrup liberally on the cake layers. Frost between the layers as well as the top and sides of the cake with dark chocolate frosting.

Hold the frosted cake in one hand over a large bowl and press the remaining chocolate chips into the sides of the frosted cake. Sprinkle chips on the top.

Chocolate Chunk Cake

Follow directions for making Deep Chip Cake. Chop 3 king-size candy bars (any flavor) into small bits and add with or instead of the chocolate chips.

Oh! Chocolate!

**Serves
12**

A totally decadent cake—only about 2 inches tall but almost solid chocolate. It contains only a tiny amount of flour so it can be consumed by people allergic to flour.

You can replace the semisweet chocolate with milk chocolate, but you will need 4 tablespoons of flour to get the milk chocolate to set up.

This cake can be expensive if you use what I think is the very finest chocolate available: Callebaut from Belgium.

5 tablespoons sweet butter
1 pound semisweet chocolate, such as Callebaut, melted and cooled
4 eggs
1 tablespoon sugar
1 tablespoon flour

Preheat oven to 425°. Cut a circle of parchment paper to fit into the bottom of a heavily buttered 8-inch cake pan.

Melt together the butter and chocolate in a microwave until the mixture is shiny and smooth. Set aside to cool.

Place the eggs and sugar in a mixer bowl. Place the bowl over boiling water and whisk the eggs with a wire whip until they are skin temperature or 98°. Don't overheat or you will have coddled eggs.

Remove egg mixture from heat and beat on high speed for 15 minutes, until the eggs are very thick and lemon colored.

Carefully fold in the flour. Gently fold into the chocolate mixture. I find the side of my hand is the best tool I own for this job.

Pour batter into the prepared cake pan and bake for exactly 15 minutes. Remove cake from the oven to cool. When cool, place it in the freezer—pan and all—for at least 12 hours.

On serving day, remove cake from the freezer. Remove the cake from the pan and place on a serving plate. (If you have trouble removing it from the pan, place it in a hot oven for 2 minutes.)

Decadent Decoration

2 cups heavy whipping cream
4 tablespoons powdered sugar
1 tablespoon vanilla
Chocolate curls (page 10)
Raspberries or strawberries

Whip heavy cream until it is frothy and add the powdered sugar and vanilla. Beat until stiff. Pile most of it in the center of the cake, and decorate with chocolate curls or fresh berries. Pipe the remaining cream around the edges of the cake. Refrigerate until served.

This cake is very intense. A little goes a long way.

Hint: If you prefer, eliminate the whipped cream and frost the cake in Chocolate Mousse Frosting (page 73) or use Chocolate Glaze (page 72).

Lemon-Lemon Cake

Serves
12 to 18

This is an exquisite cake, refreshing and tangy, perfect for summer dinner parties.

1 (18.25-ounce) box yellow cake mix
4 eggs
1 cup water
3 tablespoons lemon juice, or 2 tablespoons lemon extract
1 teaspoon grated lemon peel
½ cup vegetable or canola oil
Simple syrup, flavored with lemon juice or extract

Preheat oven to 350°. Spray two 8-inch cake pans with nonstick spray and dust lightly with flour.

Combine all ingredients in a mixer bowl and beat on low for 1 minute. Beat on high speed for 2 minutes, or until batter is very smooth.

Bake 20 to 25 minutes. Cool layers completely or freeze for 1 hour.

Lemon Frosting

2 cups whipping cream
1 tablespoon lemon juice
¼ cup powdered sugar

Whip cream until almost stiff. Add lemon juice and powdered sugar and continue beating until stiff.

Spray or brush simple syrup flavored with lemon juice or extract on the layers before frosting. Garnish the top of the cake with candied lemon slices or very thin slices of lemon dipped in fine sugar.

Mocha Almond Fudge Cake

Serves
12 to 18

A combination of white and chocolate layers, frosted in white and chocolate. The coffee extract accentuates the flavor of chocolate.

You will need two layers of chocolate cake and one layer of white (or yellow) cake. If you are using cake mix, make one box of dark chocolate layers and one layer of white (or yellow) cake. Add 1 tablespoon almond extract or amaretto and 1 tablespoon coffee extract to batter before baking. Use the Magic Cake Mix recipe (page 20) when preparing your cakes.

Before frosting, spray or brush almond-flavored simple syrup on the layers for added moisture and shelf life.

Frost the top of the cake in white frosting and the sides of the cake with chocolate frosting. Use canned frosting or follow one of my recipes to make your own.

Trim the top of the cake with chocolate curls or coffee beans.

Italian Rum Cake

Serves
12 to 18

Zuppa Iglesia is a spectacular dessert that will impress you and your guests. It is elegant and easy! This cake needs to be kept refrigerated and eaten within hours of putting it together.

1 (18.25-ounce) box French vanilla cake mix
2 (3.4-ounce) boxes French vanilla instant pudding
⅓ cup oil
½ cup water
½ cup sour cream
2 tablespoons rum flavoring
4 egg whites, beaten stiff
2 cups whipping cream
¼ cup powdered sugar
Simple syrup, flavored with 1 teaspoon of rum or rum flavoring

Preheat oven to 350°. Butter an 8-inch springform pan and dust lightly with flour.

Combine cake mix, 1 box of instant pudding, oil, water, sour cream, and 1 tablespoon rum flavoring and mix until well blended. Fold in the beaten egg whites. Pour batter into the prepared pan.

Bake the cake 30 to 40 minutes, or until the cake tests done. Remove from oven and cool completely. Freeze 1 hour.

While the cake is freezing, prepare second box of instant pudding according to directions on the box but substitute 1 cup of whipping cream for the milk.

Remove cake from the freezer and cut it in half horizontally. Spray or brush the cake liberally with simple syrup to which you have added 1 teaspoon of rum or rum flavoring.

Spoon pudding mix into the center of the cut layers. Freeze cake until set, about 30 minutes, then frost cake with remaining 1 cup of whipped cream to which you have added powdered sugar and the remaining 1 tablespoon of rum flavoring.

Hint: Replace pudding mix with Custard Cream Filling (page 53). This makes a remarkable sheetcake.

*L*iquor Cake

Serves
12 to 18

Irish whiskey, rum, bourbon, or brandy flavors this custard-filled cake. It's simple to prepare and delightful to serve.

2 frozen (8-inch) layers white or yellow cake
1 cup whiskey, rum, bourbon, or brandy
2 cups whipping cream
¼ cup powdered sugar

Custard Cream Filling

½ cup sugar
3 tablespoons flour
Pinch of salt
1 cup cream, scalded
1 egg, slightly beaten
1 teaspoon vanilla or orange flavoring

Using the top of a double boiler, combine dry ingredients with the scalded cream. Cook the mixture for 15 minutes, stirring constantly. Pour some of the hot mixture over the beaten eggs, stir, and return the mixture to the top of the double boiler. (This will prevent the eggs from coddling.) Cook mixture for 10 minutes, or until the custard is thickened.

Cool custard and add vanilla or orange flavoring.

Split frozen cake layers in half. Brush or spray liberally with the liquor. Spread the Cream Custard Filling between the layers.

Frost the top and sides of the cake with whipped cream mixed with powdered sugar. Refrigerate until served.

Hint: The easy way to prepare cream custard filling: Mix 1 small box vanilla instant pudding with 1 cup whipped cream. Fold the pudding into the whipped cream. Chill. Either way, this is a fabulous custard to fill cakes or cream puffs, or serve it in tall sherbet glasses.

Super Moist Chocolate Cake

**Serves
18**

I'll never stop collecting chocolate cake recipes. I was given this one by a wonderful lady in her nineties who lives in Montana. You'll need regular, high-calorie mayonnaise to make this work.

1 cup mayonnaise
2 cups sugar
4 eggs
1 teaspoon vanilla
2 cups flour
1 cup cocoa
1½ teaspoons plus ¼ teaspoon baking soda
⅓ cup milk
1 cup water
1 cup semisweet chocolate chips

Preheat oven to 350°. Butter and flour a 9 x 13-inch pan.

Cream together mayonnaise, sugar, eggs, and vanilla. Add flour, cocoa, baking soda, and stir to blend. Add milk and water and beat 2 minutes. Fold in chocolate chips.

Bake 30 minutes, or until cake tests done. Cool. Cover with powdered sugar or chocolate frosting.

Piña Colada Cake

Serves
12 to 18

This cake keeps moist and fresh for a long time. It will be one of your favorites. If you are a dedicated chocoholic, replace yellow cake mix with chocolate.

1 (18.25-ounce) box yellow cake mix
4 eggs
⅓ cup vegetable or canola oil
⅔ cup water
½ cup sour cream
⅓ cup dark rum
1 (3.4-ounce) box coconut cream or vanilla instant pudding
1 cup flaked coconut

Preheat oven to 350°. Butter and flour two 8-inch cake pans.

Using a mixer, combine all ingredients except coconut. When ingredients are well blended, stir in the coconut. Pour mixture into the prepared pans and bake for 25 to 30 minutes, until the cake tests done.

Cool the layers. Remove layers from the pans and frost with whipped cream or Piña Colada Frosting (page 81).

Orange Blossom Cake

Serves
12 to 18

This is a fairly dense cake that is lovely to serve at a wedding reception or a baby shower.

1 (18.25-ounce) box white cake mix
4 egg whites
⅓ cup vegetable or canola oil
1 (3.4-ounce) package orange or lemon instant pudding
¾ cup orange juice
¾ cup sour cream
Simple syrup, flavored with orange

Preheat oven to 350°. Spray two 8-inch cake pans with nonstick spray and dust lightly with flour.

Mix all the ingredients except simple syrup together until well blended. Pour batter into the prepared pans and bake 20 to 25 minutes, or until the cake tests done. Place the hot pans on a slightly damp tea towel to cool.

Freeze the layers for 1 hour then liberally spray or brush them with simple syrup with orange flavoring or orange juice. Frost with orange-flavored whipped cream.

Decorate the cake with orange blossoms or orange slices.

Sampler Cake

**Serves
12 to 18**

This is the most exciting cake you can put together. When it is cut, you can expect gasps of joy from your family and friends because there is one layer of strawberry cake, one of white cake, and the bottom layer is dark chocolate. Beautiful.

Bake 1 box each of chocolate, white, and strawberry cake mix using the Magic Cake Mix recipe (page 20) for each batch. Unless you have six cake pans you will have to bake two layers at a time. Make sure the pans are cool before reusing them.

Cool cake layers completely and freeze them for 1 hour to make frosting easy. Then brush or spray each layer with simple syrup.

Decorate between the layers with a thin layer of strawberry jam. Frost between the layers and top of the cake with vanilla frosting. Decorate the sides with chocolate frosting. Or use whipped cream frosting and decorate the top with fresh strawberries.

Refrigerate the cake until it is served if you use whipped cream.

Poppy Seed Cake

**Serves
12 to 18**

The most frequently requested cake for weddings, this recipe is simple to prepare and delicious. Remember to soak the poppy seeds in buttermilk for at least 15 minutes or they will be crunchy.

2 tablespoons poppy seeds
1 cup buttermilk
1 cup butter, softened
1 cup sugar
4 large eggs
2½ cups flour
2 teaspoons baking powder
1 teaspoon baking soda
Pinch of salt
2 tablespoons fresh lemon juice
1 tablespoon vanilla
1 teaspoon cinnamon
Simple syrup

Soak the poppy seeds in 1 cup buttermilk for at least 15 minutes, until most of the buttermilk is absorbed.

Preheat oven to 350°. Butter two 8-inch cake pans and dust lightly with flour.

Cream together the butter and sugar, and add eggs one at a time. Add dry ingredients, flavorings, and the poppy seed-buttermilk mixture. Pour batter into the prepared pans and bake 40 minutes, or until the cake tests done.

Apply simple syrup between the layers before frosting the cake with Cream Cheese Frosting (page 75) or whipped cream.

Raspberry Chocolate Trifle Cake

Serves
12 to 18

We had lunch at Max's in San Francisco one afternoon and saw this cake. These are large—about 12 inches across. You can serve twelve generous slices.

You will need two layers of dark chocolate cake, frozen and split in half. Spray or brush simple syrup on each portion of the cake.

Assemble the cake by spreading chocolate frosting and raspberry jam on the tops of each layer.

Whip 2 cups of whipping cream to which you have added ¼ cup powdered sugar and 3 tablespoons triple sec, brandy, or vanilla extract.

Spread whipped cream between the layers and on the sides of the cake. Use a pastry tube to decorate the top and bottom borders. Spread fresh raspberries on top. Keep refrigerated until served.

Hint: If you want to serve a huge cake, bake two boxes of mix, doubling the Magic Cake Mix recipe (page 20), and pour batter into three prepared 10-inch cake pans.

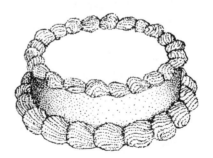

Sacher Torte

Serves
12 to 18

Sacher Torte was made famous at the Sacher Hotel in Austria. The cake is usually decorated with chocolate glaze and has the word Sacher piped in chocolate on top of the cake.

7 ounces semisweet chocolate (not chocolate chips)
½ stick sweet butter, at room temperature
8 egg yolks
1 tablespoon vanilla
10 egg whites
¾ cup extra-fine sugar
1 cup sifted flour
½ cup apricot jam
Chocolate Ganache (page 28), or 1 (16-ounce) can chocolate frosting
Chocolate Glaze (page 72)

Preheat oven to 350°. Butter two 9-inch cake pans and place a round circle of parchment or brown paper on the bottom of each pan.

Melt chocolate and butter together in the microwave. Stir the mixture and allow it to cool. Beat egg yolks until thick and lemon-colored; fold yolks and vanilla into the chocolate and butter mixture. Beat egg whites until foamy; add sugar slowly. Continue to beat egg whites until stiff.

Fold half of the egg whites into the chocolate mixture and blend carefully. Pour this mixture into the remaining egg whites. Sift flour on top and carefully fold the mixture together so that no trace of egg whites remains. Do not overmix.

Pour mixture into the prepared pans, and bake 25 to 30 minutes, or until the cake tests done. Cool the layers by placing them on a damp tea towel. Run a knife around the side of the cake to loosen it. Invert the cake layers onto a cake rack or cardboard rounds and remove the parchment paper.

Allow layers to cool completely before decorating. The layers may be frozen for 1 hour to make them easier to handle.

Assembling the Torte

Brush the crumbs off the layers. Spread the top of one layer with apricot jam and spread a layer of Chocolate Ganache or frosting between the layers using a spatula.

Refrigerate the cake for several hours, or freeze it for 1 hour. Pour Chocolate Glaze over the top.

Maple Walnut Cake

Serves
12 to 18

Maple Walnut Cake is so soul satisfying. Decorate it with a white frosting stirred with some maple syrup and press chopped walnuts onto the sides of the cake.

1 (18.25-ounce) spice cake mix
1 (3.4-ounce) box instant pudding
4 eggs
¾ cup water
⅓ cup vegetable or canola oil
¾ cup sour cream
1½ cups chopped walnuts
3 tablespoons maple syrup, or 1½ tablespoons maple flavoring
Simple syrup

Preheat oven to 350°. Butter two 8-inch cake pans and dust lightly with flour.

Using a mixer, combine cake mix, pudding, eggs, water, oil, and sour cream. Stir in the nuts and maple syrup. Pour batter into prepared cake pans and bake 25 minutes, or until the cake tests done.

Remove layers from the oven and cool them by placing the pans on a slightly damp tea towel. Spray or brush the layers with simple syrup before decorating.

Hint: This cake is delicious baked in a 9 x 13-inch pan and dusted lightly with powdered sugar.

S trawberry Amaretto Cake

Serves
12 to 18

Pretty enough for a bridal shower, sweet sixteen party, or a showstopping dessert. If you eliminate the almond flavoring, this cake is known as Pink Champagne.

The Easy Way

Add 1 tablespoon powdered strawberry gelatin to your favorite white cake mix using the Magic Cake Mix recipe (page 20).

Amaretto Frosting

2 cups whipping cream
¼ cup powdered sugar
2 tablespoons almond extract

Whip cream until frothy and add sugar and flavoring. Whip until stiff. Spread immediately on cake layers that have been brushed or sprayed with simple syrup. Frost top and sides of the cake and decorate with fresh sliced strawberries.

Carrot Cake

**Serves
18 to 24**

My carrot cake is a moist, delicious, very heavy cake that serves lots of people. This recipe also makes a great loaf cake and is fabulous for muffins.

2 cups unsifted flour
2 cups sugar (or 1½ cups fructose)
2 teaspoons baking soda
1 teaspoon salt
3 teaspoons cinnamon
4 eggs
1 cup corn oil
4 cups (8 or 9) finely grated carrots
1 cup raisins, soaked in hot water 10 minutes and drained
1 cup finely chopped walnuts, almonds, pecans, or hazelnuts

Preheat oven to 350°. Butter and flour three 8-inch cake pans and dust lightly with flour.

Mix together the flour, sugar, baking soda, salt, and cinnamon and set aside. Beat the eggs in mixer until very light and creamy. Beat in the oil gradually. Add the flour mixture and beat until smooth. Stir in the carrots, raisins, and nuts.

Pour batter into prepared pans and bake 30 minutes or until the cake tests done. Cool for 15 minutes. Remove the cake layers and continue cooling on a wire cake rack.

Freeze the layers until they are easy to handle. These layers freeze very well for a long time.

Frost the cake with Cream Cheese Frosting (page 75) or whipped cream.

Hint: Diabetics can replace the sugar with fructose. Fructose does not go directly into the bloodstream but is stored in the liver as glycogen. If you use fructose and you are preparing carrot cake for a diabetic child, I suggest you bake tiny muffins that can be included in the diet.

White Chocolate Cake

Serves
12 to 18

Those of you who love white chocolate will appreciate this delicate white cake. Be sure to separate the eggs and save the yolks for another recipe.

1 (18.25-ounce) box French vanilla cake mix
1 (3.4-ounce) box French vanilla instant pudding
4 egg whites
¼ cup water
¾ cup sour cream
⅓ cup vegetable or canola oil
3 (3.7-ounce) white chocolate candy bars, chopped into small bits
Simple syrup
2 cups heavy cream, whipped

Preheat oven to 350°. Spray two 8-inch cake pans with nonstick spray and dust lightly with flour.

Using a mixer, combine the cake mix, pudding mix, egg whites, water, sour cream, and oil and beat until smooth. Fold in the chopped white chocolate, reserving about ½ cup for decorating.

Bake the cake 20 minutes, or until it tests done. Remove layers from the oven and cool 15 minutes before inverting them onto a cake platter or cardboard. Freeze the layers for 1 hour. Remove from the freezer and brush or spray liberally with simple syrup.

Spread whipped cream between the layers and cover the top and sides with whipped cream. Pipe a border on the top and bottom edges and decorate with chunks of white chocolate.

Fat-free Chocolate Cake

Serves
12

This cake made with egg whites and nonfat yogurt is quite delicious, but should be kept refrigerated.

1 cup sifted cake flour
⅓ cup unsweetened cocoa
1 teaspoon baking soda
1 teaspoon baking powder
6 egg whites
1⅓ cups brown sugar, firmly packed
1 cup plain nonfat yogurt
1 teaspoon vanilla
Powdered sugar

Preheat oven to 350°. Spray an 8-inch square pan with nonstick spray and dust the pan with flour.

In a small bowl, mix together the flour, cocoa, baking soda, and baking powder.

Use a mixer to beat the egg whites, brown sugar, yogurt, and vanilla until well blended. Add the flour mixture and beat until just moistened.

Bake 30 to 40 minutes, or until the cake tests done. Remove the cake from the oven and allow it to cool for 10 minutes. Invert the cooled cake onto a serving platter and dust with powdered sugar. Serve warm or cool.

LUSCIOUS FROSTINGS AND SAUCES

If you want to make your own frostings, here are some great, relatively simple recipes. My favorite is the Cream Cheese Frosting. Whipped cream also makes a great cake frosting. The Chocolate Mousse Frosting is fabulous—melt-in-your-mouth delicious and not too sweet.

Gather all your ingredients before starting to make your frosting. This will make things infinitely easier.

Here's another little secret: It's expensive, but the canned ready-to-spread frostings are great. They are easy to use and the frosting stays soft on the cake for a long time. Heat a can of prepared frosting in the microwave for 45 seconds, stir, and drizzle it over cookies and cakes. Almost no one will know. If you have leftover frosting in the can, replace the plastic lid and store it in a cool cupboard for use at another time.

Have fun and don't forget to lick the bowl!

How to Frost a Cake

- After cake layers have been baked, place the hot pans on a damp tea towel and allow the layers to cool completely before removing them from the cake pans. Place the layers on a cake plate or on cardboard rounds and freeze them for at least 1 hour. It is not necessary to cover the layers unless they are going to be frozen for more than a few hours.
- After removing cakes from the freezer, place one layer rounded side down on the cake platter so that the flat side of the cake is on

the top. If the bottom of the cake is burned at all, scrape away that part using a potato peeler. Brush off any cake crumbs so that they don't get mixed into the frosting.

- Spray the cake layer with simple syrup (page 19). Spread frosting on top of the layer almost to the edge. Spray simple syrup on the second layer and place that layer flat side down on top of the bottom layer with the rounded side up. Frost the sides of the cake. You can hold the cake in one hand and apply frosting to the sides of the cake with a spatula. Place the cake back onto the cake platter and cover the top of the cake with frosting, making sure that the top frosting meets the side frosting.

- Be creative. Use a pastry tube to decorate the top and bottom edges of the cake and garnish with fresh fruit, fresh flowers, nuts, cherries, or whatever looks good. Stand back and listen to the applause!

How to Glaze a Cake

- Freeze the cake layers for at least 1 hour while you prepare the glaze. Remove layers from the freezer and brush away any loose cake crumbs.

- If you are glazing a single layer, hold it in one hand over a large bowl. Use a hand spatula (which you can buy in any cake supply store) to apply the glaze. Excess glaze will drip off the cake into the bowl. Put unused glaze into a jar and store it indefinitely in your refrigerator; reheat in a microwave for future use.

- Place the glazed cake onto a cake platter. Don't refrigerate the cake after it has been glazed or it will not harden; it will be dull, streaky, sticky, or all of the above. Allow it to harden at room temperature and store at room temperature after glazing.

- Decorate the glazed cake imaginatively and serve with pride.

Brandy Sauce

Makes
2 cups

Brandy sauce is marvelous over hot bread pudding. It can be stored for a long time refrigerated in a tightly sealed container.

1 large egg, at room temperature
⅔ stick butter
1½ cups powdered sugar
1 teaspoon vanilla
3 tablespoons brandy
1 cup whipped cream

Beat the egg until frothy and add powdered sugar, vanilla, and brandy. Cool. Fold the whipped cream carefully into the egg mixture and chill.

Easy Brandy or Rum Sauce

Makes
2 cups

Allow 1 pint of French vanilla ice cream to stand at room temperature for 15 minutes, or until it is softened. Stir in 1 tablespoon of brandy or rum and serve

Chocolate Fudge Sauce

Makes
2 cups

Although not as rich as Chocoholics ChocolateButter, this recipe makes a great sauce.

3 ounces unsweetened chocolate
1 cup brown sugar, tightly packed
½ cup light corn syrup
4 tablespoons butter
1 cup heavy cream
1 tablespoon vanilla, rum, Kahlua, or favorite liqueur

Melt the chocolate and stir in sugar, corn syrup, and butter. Simmer, stirring occasionally, about 30 minutes. Use a double boiler; it will take longer but will prevent scorching.

Beat in heavy cream and cook another 10 minutes. Stir in vanilla or liqueur. Cool and store.

Hint: This is easily reheated in a microwave.

Lowfat Hot Fudge Sauce

Makes
2 cups

½ cup cocoa
1 cup lowfat sour cream
1 cup sugar
1 teaspoon vanilla

Combine all the ingredients in the top of a double boiler. Cook over boiling water for an hour, stirring occasionally. The sauce will become thick and can be stored in the refrigerator for a long time.

Coconut Frosting

Makes
3 cups

Use this in place of the Coconut Pecan Frosting when you want a topping that is lower in cholesterol.

1 stick butter
1½ cups flaked coconut
1 cup brown sugar, firmly packed
¼ cup milk
2 cups sifted powdered sugar

Melt 2 tablespoons of the butter in a frying pan. Add all the coconut and stir until coconut is golden brown.

Remove half of the coconut and set aside. Melt the remaining butter and pour it into the frying pan with half the coconut still in it. Add brown sugar and cook, stirring constantly, for about 2 minutes, or until the mixture is well blended. Add milk and bring mixture to a boil.

Remove pan from heat and allow mixture to cool for 10 minutes. Slowly add powdered sugar, beating well after each addition until the frosting is firm enough to spread.

Spread frosting on the cake and sprinkle additional coconut on top.

Chocolate Glaze

**Makes
2 cups**

This is what we used to decorate Sacher Torte and other tortes at Chocoholics Bakery. Use the glaze lukewarm for the best results.

4 ounces semisweet chocolate, broken into small pieces
1 cup heavy cream
1 teaspoon corn syrup
¼ cup sugar
1 teaspoon vanilla

Combine chocolate, cream, corn syrup, and sugar in a saucepan and cook over low heat, stirring constantly, until the chocolate melts. Cook an additional 3 to 4 minutes. Remove mixture from heat and add vanilla. Cool to room temperature. Use over cake layers as a glaze.

Hint: This chocolate can be stored, reheated, and used at a later time.

Ultimate Chocolate Frosting

**Makes
2 cups**

If you are a chocolate purist, you will enjoy making this frosting.

4 ounces unsweetened chocolate, melted and cooled
3 egg whites
1½ cups powdered sugar
2 sticks butter, at room temperature

Melt the unsweetened chocolate in the microwave. Set aside to cool.

Beat egg whites until almost stiff and add powdered sugar, a little at a time. Beat the egg white mixture until stiff.

In another bowl, cream the butter until it is smooth and soft. Add the egg white mixture to the butter, beating constantly. Add melted chocolate and continue to beat until frosting is thick enough to spread.

Chocolate Mousse Frosting

Makes
3 cups

This is a new frosting I developed especially for this cookbook. It is rich and creamy, not too sweet, and very simple to prepare. It is also spectacular served as mousse in tall glasses.

2 ounces unsweetened chocolate, melted and cooled
14 ounces (1 can) sweetened condensed milk
½ cup cold water
1 (3.4-ounce) package chocolate instant pudding
1 cup heavy cream, whipped

Beat together the melted, cooled chocolate and the sweetened condensed milk. Gradually add water and instant pudding; mix until smooth. Fold in the whipped cream. Use it as cake frosting immediately, or spoon it into eight flute glasses and chill for at least 1 hour before serving as mousse.

Hint: Whip the cream before you melt the chocolate. Scrape whipped cream into a bowl and use the original bowl in which you whipped the cream to complete the frosting. No need to wash the beater and bowl.

Cooked Buttercream Frosting

Makes
2½ cups

Rainy days make this frosting difficult to prepare because of the moisture in the air. Make it on a dry day and the result is very creamy and smooth.

¾ cup extra-fine sugar
½ cup water
⅛ teaspoon cream of tartar
3 sticks butter, at room
   temperature

5 large egg yolks
4 ounces semisweet chocolate,
   melted and cooled
1 tablespoon liqueur, or 1
   tablespoon vanilla

Cook sugar, water, and cream of tartar in a saucepan until the sugar is melted and the mixture comes to a boil. Continue to cook until the temperature reaches 240° on a candy thermometer. If crystals appear on the sides of the pan, wash them down using a damp pastry brush. This will prevent the frosting from becoming grainy.

Cream the butter while the syrup is cooking. In separate bowl, beat the egg yolks until they are very thick and lemon-colored. Continue to beat the yolks as you pour the hot sugar syrup into them. Beat until cool. Add the melted chocolate and flavoring.

Add the butter to the sugar-egg mixture and beat only until well blended. Use immediately.

Mocha Buttercream Frosting

Makes
2½ cups

This is much easier than cooking the syrup for Cooked Buttercream Frosting. It keeps well and is not overly sweet.

1 cup sugar
⅓ cup boiling water
6 ounces semisweet chocolate, or
   1 cup semisweet chocolate
   chips

2 sticks plus 2 tablespoons sweet
   butter, at room temperature
3 egg yolks
2 teaspoons instant coffee
⅔ cup powdered sugar

Combine the sugar, water, and chocolate in a saucepan and heat and stir until just melted. Set aside to cool.

Cream butter until light and fluffy. Beat in the egg yolks one at a time, add coffee and mix until well blended. Gradually add powdered sugar. Stir in the chocolate mixture and blend thoroughly.

Cream Cheese Frosting

Makes
3 cups

This is a lovely creamy frosting—perfect on carrot and zucchini cakes and it works well as wedding cake frosting.

1 (8-ounce) package cream cheese, at room temperature
½ stick butter, at room temperature
2 cups powdered sugar
1 tablespoon lemon juice or extract
1 teaspoon vanilla

Blend all ingredients until light and creamy. Scrape down the sides and bottom of the mixing bowl so no clumps of cheese remain. Spread frosting between the layers and on the top and sides of the cake.

Hint: Garnish with nuts, fruit, or flowers.

Chocolate Cream Cheese Frosting

Follow recipe for Cream Cheese Frosting, eliminating the lemon extract. Melt and cool 4 ounces of semisweet chocolate and blend the chocolate into the frosting. Easy and delicious.

Hint: For bittersweet chocolate frosting, use 2 ounces of unsweetened chocolate to replace the semisweet chocolate.

Caramel Sauce

Makes
2 cups

This sauce is quite sweet and wonderful over ice cream or used as a mix-in for cakes or brownies.

1¼ cups sugar
½ cup corn syrup
Pinch of salt
⅓ cup heavy cream

Use a heavy saucepan to heat the sugar until it becomes liquid and no lumps remain. Stir constantly. Cook until the sugar is light brown in color.

Slowly pour in corn syrup and salt and beat with a wire whisk. Add cream slowly. If sauce is too thick, add an additional tablespoonful of cream.

Chocolate Caramel Sauce

Makes
2 cups

1 cup brown sugar, tightly packed
3 tablespoons water
1 tablespoon butter
¼ cup chocolate syrup
1 teaspoon vanilla
1 tablespoon cornstarch
1 cup hot water

Cook brown sugar and water until it becomes a light brown color. Remove from heat. Mix butter, chocolate syrup, vanilla, and cornstarch into a paste and add the hot water. Cook until the mixture reaches 220° on a candy thermometer. This will take about 15 minutes; stir it constantly. When sauce is thick, remove from heat.

Maple Walnut Sauce

Makes
1½ cups

You can serve this over French toast, waffles, or ice cream.

1 cup maple syrup
½ cup chopped walnuts
1 teaspoon lemon juice
1 teaspoon rum flavoring

Warm syrup in microwave. Stir in walnuts, lemon juice, and rum flavoring. Serve warm or cold. Store indefinitely in your refrigerator.

Chocolate Sour Cream Frosting

Makes
2 cups

This is the easiest and smoothest frosting you can make. If you like a lot of frosting, double this recipe.

1 stick butter, at room temperature
4 ounces unsweetened chocolate, melted and cooled
4 cups powdered sugar
1 cup sour cream
1 tablespoon vanilla

Cream butter until light and fluffy. Add chocolate and blend well. Add powdered sugar. Sift the sugar if it is lumpy. You can use a strainer to do this. Blend in sour cream and vanilla. The more you whip this frosting, the thicker it will become.

Lemon Curd

Makes
3 cups

Lemon Curd is thick and tart and tastes like the best lemon pie filling in the world. You can buy expensive jars of this wonderful stuff in gourmet shops, but it's very simple to make. Using your imagination you can create some fabulous treats.

Lemon curd can be used as a pie filling or as a spread. Mixed one-to-one with whipped cream, it can be used as a filling for tarts and pies. The recipe was given to me by my friend Lolita Leen.

1 stick sweet butter, at room temperature
½ cup fresh lemon juice
Grated peel of 1 large lemon
1½ cups sugar
Pinch of salt
3 egg yolks
3 large eggs

Use a double boiler to melt the butter and stir in the lemon juice, grated lemon peel, sugar, and salt. Slightly beat the egg yolks together with the whole eggs and add this to the butter-sugar mixture.

Cook mixture over medium heat about 30 minutes; use a wire whisk to stir until thickened. You can use a heavy saucepan but it has been my experience that lemon curd scorches easily; I suggest using the double boiler.

Hints:

You can replace the fresh lemon juice with bottled lemon juice.

If you use a fresh lemon, roll the lemon on your counter until it is soft. You'll get more juice.

To simplify grating the lemon, freeze the lemon rind for 30 minutes and it will be easier to grate.

Coconut Pecan Frosting

Makes
3 cups

This frosting is great on German Chocolate Cake. The canned version is extremely sweet but because it's easier, it is what most bakeries use.

I spooned a cup of this frosting in a circle around the center of a Bundt cake before baking it. The result was a cake with a creamy center.

1 cup evaporated milk
1 cup sugar
3 egg yolks
1 stick butter, at room temperature

1 tablespoon vanilla
2 cups flaked coconut
1 cup chopped pecans

Combine evaporated milk, sugar, egg yolks, and butter in a saucepan. Stir and cook over medium heat until thickened, about 12 minutes (or use a double boiler which takes much longer but doesn't require all your attention).

Remove mixture from heat. Cool for 5 minutes and add vanilla, coconut, and chopped pecans.

Hints: You may need additional coconut if the frosting isn't thick enough, so have some extra available.

Make a double batch—this is good enough to eat with a spoon, it's marvelous as a frosting for cupcakes, and it's even good over ice cream! It will keep in a tightly capped jar in your refrigerator for months.

Easy Coconut Pecan Frosting

Makes
2 cups

This requires no cooking; it is not as rich as the cooked version, but it's great if you are in a hurry.

1 (3.4-ounce) package butter
   pecan or vanilla instant pudding
1 cup evaporated milk

¼ cup light corn syrup
1½ cups flaked coconut
1 cup chopped pecans

Use a fork to blend the instant pudding, evaporated milk, and corn syrup together. Add coconut and pecans. Chill ½ hour. Use for filling and top of one German Chocolate or Butter Pecan Cake.

Fruit Curd

Makes
2 cups

Once I discovered how easy it was to make lemon curd, I began to experiment using other fresh fruit juices and frozen juice concentrate. I learned that it is possible to create as many fruit-flavored curds as there are juices. Fruit curds make a marvelous filling for a split angel food cake or a layer of white or yellow cake.

1 stick butter, melted
½ cup sugar
4 ounces frozen juice concentrate (lemon, grape, orange, papaya)
2 whole eggs
4 egg yolks

Place the top of the boiler over boiling water and whisk together the butter, sugar and fruit juice concentrate.

In a separate bowl, whisk together the eggs and egg yolks. Add a little of the hot mixture to the egg yolks to prevent them from curdling. Then add the eggs to the hot mixture in the top of the double boiler, whisking ingredients together until they are smooth.

Continue heating over medium heat until the mixture thickens. Spoon the curd into a tightly capped jar and refrigerate. This should keep for at least a month.

Hint: If you combine these fruit curds with whipped cream and spoon the mixture into long-stemmed glasses, you have an elegant dessert—fast and easy. These curds also make great pie and tart fillings.

Piña Colada Frosting

Makes
3 cups

1 (20-ounce) can crushed pineapple, drained of its juice
1 (3.4-ounce) package coconut cream or vanilla instant pudding
⅓ cup dark rum
1 (16-ounce) container whipped topping

Combine all the ingredients except whipped topping in a bowl and beat until well blended. Fold in the whipped topping.

Red Raspberry Sauce

Makes
2 cups

This sauce can be made with a variety of fresh or frozen fruits. Simple to prepare, there is no cooking required. It is tart and delicious on ice cream.

20 ounces (2 packages) frozen raspberries packed in syrup
Juice of 1 lemon

Defrost the raspberries unopened in a deep bowl. Using a food processor with a steel blade, combine raspberries and lemon juice; process until smooth.

Hint: If you don't want the seeds, press the mixture through a strainer.

*W*hipped Cream Frosting

Makes
4 cups

Whipped cream frosting delights everyone, even people who don't like frosting. It's easy to prepare and although it needs to be kept refrigerated until it is served, it holds up surprisingly well at room temperature.

I freeze wedding cakes with whipped cream frosting for at least an hour so they will hold up for several hours during the wedding reception. You can freeze decorated cake layers longer if you like, but remember it will take longer to defrost at room temperature so plan accordingly.

2 cups whipping cream
¼ cup powdered sugar

Beat the cream until it is frothy and add sugar slowly. Beat until stiff and use immediately to frost the sides and top of one 8-inch, two-layer cake.

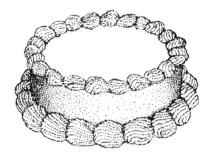

$\mathscr{D}$ECADENT $\mathscr{C}$HEESECAKES

The cheesecakes that we developed at Chocoholics Bakery were the first commercially produced cheesecakes in Humboldt County, California. They were 3 inches tall and sometimes taller. We could make 150 different flavors!

Almost everyone loves cheesecake. They are easy to prepare and can be elegant when decorated with fresh fruits, whipped cream, or drizzled chocolate sauce.

Hints for Perfect Cheesecakes

- Always beat the cream cheese until it is very smooth. Use a spatula to scrape down the mixing bowl so that no lumps of cheese remain in the batter. These lumps do not dissolve when the cheesecake bakes.
- If you can find cream cheese with no additives, it is worth the extra money. You will have a cheesecake that is fantastic instead of just marvelous.
- Once you add the eggs, take care not to overbeat or the cheesecake will be tough.
- Don't worry if the top cracks; this is a sign that the cheesecake is thoroughly baked. Cover the cracks with whipped cream, chocolate frosting, sour cream, or fresh fruit.
- Chocolate cheesecakes require the addition of 4 ounces of melted and cooled bittersweet or semisweet chocolate plus 4 tablespoons of whipping cream, half-and-half, or melted butter to prevent dryness.

- For a marbling effect, swirl 2 ounces of melted and cooled chocolate into the batter which has been poured into a prepared springform pan.
- You can also swirl jelly or jam into the prepared batter, and of course, Chocoholics ChocolateButter is easy and delicious added to the batter or drizzled over the final product. Spoon a little warm sauce onto the dessert plate for a picture-perfect dessert.
- Place a cookie sheet covered with foil under the filled springform pan before baking to prevent leakage, unless you use a *bain-marie* (water bath). I cover the sides of my springform pan with foil before placing it in the water bath or on a cookie sheet.
- You can cover your baked and cooled cheesecake with foil and store it in the refrigerator up to 2 weeks before serving. You can remove the cakes from the springform pan, cover, and freeze them for 3 months before serving.

Cream Cheese Cheesecake

**Serves
12 to 18**

The 150 different cheesecakes that we created at the bakery were all variations on this recipe. This cheesecake is very dense and rich. It has to be kept refrigerated and is lovely served with fresh fruit in season, especially strawberries or blueberries.

5 (8-ounce) packages cream cheese, at room temperature
1¾ cups sugar
3 tablespoons flour
¼ cup whipping cream
1 tablespoon vanilla
5 eggs

Preheat oven to 500°. Butter a 10-inch springform pan and press a graham cracker crust or cookie crumb crust into the bottom of the pan.

Use a mixer to cream together the cream cheese, sugar, flour, whipping cream, and vanilla. Add the eggs, one at a time, and beat until smooth. Use a spatula to scrape down the cream cheese at the bottom of the bowl so no lumps of cheese remain in the batter.

Pour mixture into the prepared crust and bake 10 minutes. Reduce the oven temperature to 200° and bake 1 hour. Turn the oven off and leave cheesecake in the oven overnight with the door slightly open, or cool it out of a draft for 1 to 2 hours. When the cheesecake is completely cool, refrigerate it for 4 hours or overnight before serving. Decorate with whipped cream or fresh fruit if desired.

Basic Cheesecake

Serves
12 to 18

You will be able to create untold numbers of cheesecakes using this basic recipe and your imagination. Enjoy!

Basic Graham Cracker Crust

1½ cups graham cracker or cookie crumbs
1 stick melted butter
1 tablespoon powdered sugar

Mix together the crumbs, melted butter, and sugar and press into the bottom of a buttered 8- or 9-inch springform pan.

Hint: For a crunchy crust, bake crust at 350° for 10 minutes. Remove the crust from the oven and prepare the filling while the crust cools.

Basic Filling

3 (8-ounce) packages cream cheese, at room temperature
1 cup sugar
5 tablespoons sour cream
1 tablespoon vanilla
4 eggs, beaten

Beat the cream cheese, sugar, sour cream, and vanilla for about 15 minutes, or until the mixture is very light and fluffy.

Add the beaten eggs and mix until just blended. Do not overbeat eggs in the cheese mixture; it makes cheesecake heavy and dry.

Pour the cheese mixture into the prepared crust and bake the cheesecake at 350° for 30 minutes. Turn the oven off and leave the cheesecake in the oven for 30 minutes with the oven door closed. Remove the cheesecake from the oven and use the following Sour Cream Topping, or refrigerate 4 hours or overnight before decorating.

Sour Cream Topping

The tops of cheesecakes tend to crack after baking. This topping improves the appearance of a cracked cheesecake.

1 pint minus 5 tablespoons sour cream
½ cup sugar
1 tablespoon vanilla

Mix the sour cream with sugar and vanilla. Spread mixture onto the slightly cooled cheesecake. Return the sour cream–topped cheesecake to the hot oven for 5 minutes. Cool the cheesecake in the refrigerator for 8 hours before serving.

Brandied Apricot Cheesecake

Add 4 tablespoons brandy to the Basic Cheesecake recipe after mixing in the eggs. When the cheesecake is baked and cooled, spread apricot jam on top and decorate edges with whipped cream.

Cherry Cheesecake

Top the baked and cooled Basic Cheesecake with a can of cherry pie filling. Decorate edges with whipped cream.

Strawberry Amaretto Cheesecake

Add 2 tablespoons amaretto flavoring, or ¼ cup amaretto liqueur, to the Basic Cheesecake recipe. When the cheesecake is baked and cooled, decorate the top with strawberry jam or fresh strawberries.

Raspberry Cheesecake

Add 2 tablespoons powdered raspberry gelatin to the Basic Cheesecake recipe. Bake and cool. Spread raspberry jam or whipped cream and fresh raspberries on top. Decorate the edges with whipped cream.

New York–Style Cheesecake

Serves
12

You will need an 8-inch, 1-piece cake pan that is 3 inches deep and a pan about 10 inches wide and 3 inches deep, such as a large roasting pan. This cheesecake takes 3 hours of oven time to bake.

3 (8-ounce) packages cream cheese, at room temperature
½ cup sour cream
2 tablespoons cornstarch
4 eggs
3 tablespoons fresh lemon juice, or 1 tablespoon lemon extract
1 teaspoon grated lemon peel

Preheat oven to 300°. Heavily butter the sides and bottom of the 8-inch pan.

Use a mixer to blend together the cream cheese, sour cream, and cornstarch. Mix until very creamy. Add the eggs, one at a time, and add lemon flavoring and lemon peel. Be careful not to overbeat.

Pour batter into the prepared pan. Place the 8-inch pan into the larger pan. Place both pans in the oven and pour hot water into the larger pan to reach halfway up the side of the 8-inch pan. (This is called a water bath or *bain-marie*.)

Bake 2 hours. Don't peek. At the end of 2 hours, turn off the oven for 1 hour. Resist the temptation to open the oven door.

Remove the 8-inch pan from its water bath and place it on a dry towel for 10 minutes. Loosen the cheesecake from the pan by gently rotating the pan every few minutes.

When cool, invert the cheesecake onto a cardboard cake round or serving plate. Mark into 12 sections. Use a strand of dental floss to cut through the cheesecake. Serve warm, chilled, or frozen.

Hint: If you want a more tart flavor, add additional lemon flavoring. Decorate it with lemon slices.

Chocolate Mandarin Orange Cheesecake

Use the New York–Style Cheesecake recipe. Replace the lemon rind with orange rind and lemon juice with orange juice. Melt and cool 4 ounces of semisweet chocolate and swirl the chocolate into the batter. Decorate the top of the finished cheesecake with canned mandarin orange sections or candied orange peel.

Mocha Almond Fudge Cheesecake

Use the New York–Style Cheesecake recipe. Eliminate the lemon juice or extract and lemon peel; add 1 tablespoon coffee extract and 1 tablespoon almond extract to the batter. Pour batter into the prepared pan and swirl in 4 ounces bittersweet or semisweet chocolate.

Raspberry Swirl Cheesecake

Use the New York–Style Cheesecake recipe, replacing the lemon flavor with raspberry extract. Swirl ½ cup of raspberry jam into the prepared batter. Decorate the top of the finished cheesecake with fresh raspberries.

Chocoholics Cheesecake

This is a fairly complicated recipe but the result is truly dazzling. Make a batch of New York–Style Cheesecake. Heavily butter an 8-inch pan and pour one third of the batter into the bottom of the pan. Freeze the batter for 1 hour while you melt 2 ounces of semisweet chocolate; add the melted chocolate to one third of the original batter. Pour this on top of the first layer and freeze the cheesecake for another hour.

Melt 2 ounces of unsweetened chocolate and stir it into the remaining third of cheesecake batter. Pour this onto the top of the two layers and proceed with the instructions for New York–Style Cheesecake.

Mocha Marble Cheesecake

Serves
12 to 18

Just when I was convinced that the cheesecakes we made at Chocoholics Bakery were the best in the world, Bill and I had dinner at one of the Peasant Restaurants in Atlanta, Georgia. We ordered this cheesecake as dessert. The owners were gracious enough to send me the recipe.

Chocolate Crumb Crust

1 (14-ounce) package of chocolate wafers, crushed into crumbs
1 stick butter, melted

Preheat oven to 350°. Lightly butter a 10-inch springform pan. Mix together the chocolate crumbs and butter and press the mixture into the sides and the bottom of the springform pan. Bake crust 10 minutes and allow to cool while you prepare the filling.

Mocha Marble Filling

4 (8-ounce) packages cream cheese, at room temperature
½ cup hot coffee
Pinch of salt
1½ cups sugar
¾ cup flour
6 eggs
1 teaspoon vanilla
2 cups whipped cream
8 ounces semisweet chocolate, melted and cooled

Preheat oven to 350°. Use a mixer to cream the cheese until it is very smooth. Add hot coffee and salt and mix until smooth.

Add sugar and flour and beat until smooth. Add eggs and vanilla. Fold whipped cream carefully into the batter and pour batter into the prepared crust.

Swirl melted chocolate through the batter using a knife or large spoon.

Wrap the sides and bottom of the springform pan in foil and place it in a roasting pan. Place both pans into the oven and then pour enough boiling water into the larger pan to reach a quarter of the depth of the springform.

Bake 1 hour. Turn the oven off and allow the cheesecake to remain in the oven with the door closed for an additional hour.

Remove from oven and allow to cool at least 4 hours. Chill the cheesecake and serve.

Hint: If desired, cover top with whipped cream and shaved chocolate before serving.

Very Rich Cheesecake

**Serves
12 to 18**

This is a fabulous cheesecake, easy to prepare and marvelous to serve. You can vary the flavorings and even the crust and always be assured of a great dessert.

1½ cups finely ground, toasted almonds
4 (8-ounce) packages cream cheese, at room temperature
1½ cups sugar
1 (16-ounce) container sour cream
1 tablespoon vanilla
2 tablespoons fresh lemon juice
6 large eggs

Preheat oven to 325°. Butter a 9-inch springform pan and sprinkle ½ cup of the almonds into the bottom of the pan.

Cream the cheese until it is very smooth. Make sure there are no lumps in the bottom of the mixing bowl. Add sugar and continue beating until the mixture is light and fluffy. Add the sour cream and flavorings.

Add eggs, one at a time, being careful not to overbeat. Stir in the remaining almonds by hand. Pour batter into the prepared pan.

Place the cheesecake on a cookie sheet covered in foil in the center of your oven and bake 45 to 60 minutes, or until set. Let the cheesecake rest in the oven with the heat turned off for 1 hour. Keep the door slightly open. Refrigerate the baked cheesecake for at least 4 hours before decorating and serving.

German Chocolate Cheesecake

Fold 4 ounces of melted and cooled sweet chocolate or milk chocolate into the Very Rich Cheesecake batter. Add ¼ cup heavy cream or sour cream. After the cheesecake is baked and cooled, spread Coconut Pecan Frosting (page 79) over the top.

Decorate the frosted cheesecake with pecan halves. Pipe chocolate decorations around the top border. Refrigerate until served.

Kahlua Cheesecake

Use the Very Rich Cheesecake recipe. Add 4 ounces of melted and cooled unsweetened chocolate to the batter plus ¼ cup coffee-flavored liqueur or very strong coffee.

After the cheesecake is baked and cooled, spread sweetened whipped cream over the top and decorate with candy or real coffee beans. Refrigerate until served.

Rum Pumpkin Cheesecake

Use the Very Rich Cheesecake recipe. Substitute tightly packed brown sugar for the white sugar. Add 1 cup of cooked or canned mashed pumpkin, 1 tablespoon cinnamon, 1 tablespoon ginger, 2 tablespoons rum or rum flavoring, 1 teaspoon allspice, and 1 teaspoon nutmeg to the batter.

After the cheesecake is baked and cooled, spread sweetened whipped cream over the top. Sprinkle cinnamon and sugar lightly over cream. Refrigerate until served.

Chocolate Turtle Cheesecake

**Serves
12 to 18**

I received this fabulous recipe from a multitalented young lady, Ann Leen. If you like caramel, you'll love this. Everyone in my family did.

Vanilla Crumb Crust

2 cups vanilla wafer crumbs
¾ stick butter, melted

Preheat oven to 350°. Butter a 9-inch springform pan. Combine the wafer crumbs and butter and press crust into the bottom of the buttered pan. Bake 10 minutes. Remove pan from the oven and cool.

Caramel Filling

1 (14-ounce) bag of caramels, unwrapped
1 (5-ounce) can evaporated milk
1 cup chopped pecans
3 (8-ounce) packages cream cheese, at room temperature
½ cup sugar
1 teaspoon vanilla
2 eggs
½ cup semisweet chocolate chips, melted

Preheat oven to 350°. Using the top of a double boiler, melt the caramels and the evaporated milk. Stir until smooth. Pour caramel mixture over the prepared crust. Top caramel with chopped pecans.

Combine cream cheese, sugar, and vanilla and beat together until well blended, making sure to scrape down the bowl several times. Add the eggs, one at a time, beating until just mixed. Stir in the melted chocolate and pour the cream cheese mixture over the caramel and pecans.

Bake 40 minutes. Chill overnight before serving.

Hint: To take the easy way, substitute 8 ounces of the apple-dipping caramel found in the produce department at the grocery store for the bag of caramels and evaporated milk.

*W*hite Chocolate Cheesecake

Serves
12 to 18

Lovers of white chocolate, this one is for you!

4 (8-ounce) packages cream cheese, at room temperature
1½ cups sugar
1 (16-ounce) container sour cream
3 tablespoons flour
1 tablespoon vanilla
6 egg whites
2 cups white chocolate chips

White Chocolate Topping

1 cup whipped topping
3 (3.7-ounce) white chocolate candy bars, broken into squares

Preheat oven to 325° and butter a 9-inch springform pan. Press a vanilla cookie crumb crust (page 94) into the bottom of the pan and bake crust 10 minutes.

Cream the cheese until it is very light and fluffy. Add the sugar, sour cream, flour, and vanilla and continue beating until the cheese is very smooth. Add egg whites and beat until they are just incorporated. Fold in white chocolate chips.

Place the cheesecake on a cookie sheet and bake 45 to 60 minutes, or until cheesecake is set.

Turn off the oven and let the cheesecake remain in the oven for 1 hour. Keep the oven door open slightly. When the cheesecake is cooled completely, remove the springform. Decorate the top of the cheesecake with the whipped topping and chunks of white chocolate candy bars.

Chocolate Cheesecake

Serves
12 to 18

This cheesecake can only be described as heavenly!

Chocolate Crust

24 chocolate wafers
¾ stick butter, melted
¼ teaspoon cinnamon

Crush chocolate wafers and stir in melted butter and cinnamon. Mix the crumbs and butter together and press crust into the bottom of a greased 9-inch springform pan. Chill.

Chocolate Filling

3 (8-ounce) packages cream cheese, at room temperature
1 cup sugar
8 ounces semisweet chocolate, melted and cooled
2 teaspoons cocoa
1 tablespoon vanilla or Kahlua
3 eggs
1 cup sour cream

Preheat oven to 350°. Use mixer to combine cream cheese and sugar and beat until light and fluffy. Scrape the bowl so no lumps of cheese remain.

Stir in the chocolate, cocoa, and vanilla (or Kahlua). Add the eggs one at a time. Add sour cream and continue to beat until very smooth and well blended.

Pour batter into the prepared crust and bake for 1 hour and 10 minutes. The cheesecake may appear soft, but it will harden as it cools.

Cool the cheesecake at room temperature and chill it for at least 5 hours. Garnish with whipped cream.

Fudge Truffle Cheesecake

Serves
12 to 18

A very simple, rich, and luscious cheesecake that will please everyone.

Fudge Filling

2 cups semisweet chocolate chips, or 12 ounces semisweet chocolate
    broken into small pieces
3 (8-ounce) packages cream cheese, at room temperature
1 (14-ounce) can sweetened condensed milk
1 tablespoon vanilla

Preheat oven to 350°. Line the bottom of a buttered 9-inch springform
pan with a cookie crumb crust.

Microwave the chocolate until melted. Set aside to cool.

Beat the cream cheese until light and fluffy. Add sweetened condensed milk and blend until smooth. Scrape down the mixer bowl so
no chunks of cheese remain. Add vanilla and the melted, cooled chocolate and mix until well blended.

Pour the filling into the prepared crust and bake 1 hour, or until
center of the cheesecake is set.

When the cheesecake is completely cool, refrigerate it for 4 hours
or overnight before serving. Decorate with whipped cream or fresh
flowers if desired.

Oreo Cookie Cheesecake

Serves
12 to 18

If you want the pieces of cookies incorporated into the cheesecake, break the cookies into chunks. If you want the cookies to float to the top of the cheesecake, use a food processor to grind them into fine crumbs.

Oreo Crust

1 (16-ounce) package Oreo cookies
1 stick butter, melted and cooled

Preheat oven to 350°. Spray a 9-inch springform pan with nonstick spray. Use a food processor to crush the cookies or place cookies in a plastic bag and use a rolling pin to crumble the cookies. Mix half of the crumbs with melted butter and press into the bottom of the prepared springform pan. Refrigerate while preparing the filling.

Cream Cheese Filling

4 (8-ounce) packages cream cheese, at room temperature
1 cup sugar
⅓ cup whipping cream
6 eggs
3 tablespoons flour
2 tablespoons vanilla

Use a mixer to combine the cream cheese with the sugar and whipping cream; mix until no lumps remain in the batter. Add eggs, flour, and vanilla and beat until just smooth.

Pour half of the filling over the prepared crust and scatter the remaining cookie crumbs over the top. Pour remaining filling over the cookie crumbs.

Bake until the cheesecake is golden on top and the center is almost solid, about 1 hour and 15 minutes.

Remove cheesecake from the oven and allow to cool. Run a table knife around the outside edge of the cheesecake to loosen cake from the pan. Remove the springform and place cake on a serving platter. Decorate the cheesecake with whipped cream and Oreo cookies.

Hint: This cake is best if it is allowed to cool in the refrigerator overnight.

Reduced-Calorie Cheesecake

Serves
12

The combination of fat-free or low-calorie cottage cheese, low-calorie cream cheese, and fat-free or low-calorie sour cream makes this cheesecake a little lighter. The melted butter will give your cheesecake a smoother consistency; fat-free margarine doesn't work in this recipe.

Flavor this cheesecake with lemon juice, orange juice, Kahlua, amaretto, or your favorite liqueur.

Low-Cal Filling

1 (16-ounce) container lowfat cottage cheese, at room temperature
2 (8-ounce) packages lowfat cream cheese, cubed, at room temperature
1½ cups sugar
⅓ cup cornstarch
1 (16-ounce) container lowfat sour cream
1 stick butter, melted
2 tablespoons lemon juice
1 tablespoon vanilla
1 tablespoon Kahlua
3 eggs, slightly beaten, or egg substitute

Prepare any crust you like and press it into a greased 9-inch spring-form pan.

Preheat oven to 325°. Butter a 9-inch springform pan. If cottage cheese is not already whipped, process until smooth using a food processor or a blender.

Use a mixer to combine the whipped cottage cheese, cubed cream cheese, sugar, and corn starch and beat on high speed until very smooth. Add sour cream and melted butter. Mix in lemon juice, vanilla, and Kahlua. Add the eggs last and don't overbeat.

Pour the mixture into the prepared crust and cover the sides and bottom of the pan with foil. Place the pan into a larger pan. Place both pans in the oven and pour 2 inches of boiling water into the larger pan.

Bake 1 hour and 10 minutes or until the cheesecake is firm around the edges. Turn off the oven and allow the cheesecake to cool in the oven with the door slightly open for 2 hours. Remove, cool, and refrigerate.

BLISSFUL BROWNIES

$\mathscr{I}$ am mad for brownies. They are quick and simple to make and can be filled with a magnificent variety of goodies—dark chocolate chips, crunchy nuts, white chocolate chunks, bananas, gooey marshmallow creme—whatever you desire! There's even a recipe here for brownie cupcakes filled with peanut butter and chocolate.

Brownies can be cut into any size that you please and are great to take along in lunches or on picnics. They're wonderful with a glass of cold milk for a midnight snack. They can also double as an impressive dessert—serve them topped with ice cream and drizzled with chocolate or caramel sauce for a grand finale.

The following are tried-and-true recipes we used at the bakery. I'm sure you'll find a favorite treat to satisfy your every craving.

World's Best Brownies

Makes
24 1½ x 3¼-
inch brownies

These brownies will make you famous.

5 ounces unsweetened chocolate, melted and cooled
1½ sticks butter, at room temperature
4 eggs
Pinch of salt
2 cups sugar
1 tablespoon instant coffee
1 tablespoon vanilla
1 cup sifted flour
2 cups chopped nuts

Preheat oven to 400°. Butter a 9 x 13-inch pan and dust lightly with flour. Melt the chocolate and butter together; set aside to cool. In another bowl, beat the eggs and salt until thick and lemon-colored, about 5 minutes. Add the sugar and coffee.

Add vanilla to the chocolate-butter mixture. Add this mixture to the eggs and mix just enough to blend. Add the flour using the lowest speed on the mixer and beating as little as possible. Add the nuts. Spread evenly in the prepared pan. Bake 20 to 22 minutes. A toothpick inserted in the center should come out barely dry. Brownies need to be moist; don't overbake.

Remove the pan from the oven and cool. Invert the brownies onto a serving plate. After 10 to 15 minutes, invert them again onto another plate. Cool completely and cut into squares.

Hint: I used to wrap these in clear plastic wrap to keep them very moist.

Lowfat Brownies

Makes
24 1½ x 3¼-
inch brownies

This recipe comes from my children, Daniel and Toni. These brownies are almost fat-free and as good if not better than any of the commercial varieties—and a great deal less expensive.

1 (18.25-ounce) box lowfat brownie mix
½ cup water
8 ounces plain nonfat yogurt

Preheat oven to 325°. Spray a 9 x 13-inch baking pan lightly with vegetable spray and dust lightly with flour.

Combine the brownie mix, water, and yogurt; mix together with a fork until just blended. Spread into the prepared pan and bake 30 minutes, or until brownies test done.

White Chocolate Blondies

Makes
18 1½ x 3-inch
brownies

Here's a brownie for lovers of white chocolate. They must not be over-baked or they become very dry.

1¼ stick butter, at room temperature
12 ounces white chocolate
1 cup sugar
3 large eggs
1 teaspoon vanilla
1¼ cup flour
½ teaspoon baking powder
½ cup chopped pecans

Preheat oven to 350°. Spray a 9-inch square baking pan with nonstick spray and dust lightly with flour.

Use the top of a double boiler. Combine half the butter and half the white chocolate and melt together. Stir until smooth. Remove the chocolate-butter mixture from heat and blend in the sugar, eggs, and vanilla. Stir in flour and baking powder. Add the chopped pecans.

Spread batter into the prepared pan and bake 25 minutes, or until the brownies are a light golden brown. Do not overbake.

Melt the remaining butter and white chocolate in the top of a double boiler and spread melted chocolate over the cooled brownies. When the chocolate is set, cut the brownies into bars.

Banana Fudge Brownies

Makes
16 2 x 2-inch
brownies

Just when I think I have made the perfect brownie, along comes a new recipe that is superb like this one. The brownies are heavy, moist, and delicious.

½ stick butter
1 cup semisweet chocolate chips
¾ cup flour
½ cup sugar
1 large very ripe banana, mashed
1 teaspoon vanilla
¼ teaspoon baking powder
Pinch of salt
1 large egg

Preheat oven to 350°. Butter an 8-inch square baking pan and dust lightly with flour.

Melt the butter and chocolate chips together in the microwave and stir until smooth. Set aside to cool.

Beat all the ingredients together, including the chocolate-butter mixture, and pour batter into the prepared pan.

Bake 30 minutes, or until the cake tests done. Cool and slice into squares.

Hint: Add ½ cup of chopped nuts to the batter if you choose, or sprinkle them on top of the brownies.

Peanut Butter Brownie Cupcakes

Makes
18 cupcakes

These are a big treat—for children and adults. The trick is to unwrap a small Reese's peanut butter cup and insert it in the center of the brownie, not in your mouth, before baking the cupcake.

1 (18.25-ounce) box brownie mix or 1 (18.25-ounce) German
   chocolate cake mix
18 miniature Reese's peanut butter cups

Preheat oven to 350°. Line a cupcake or muffin tin with paper liners. Unwrap the candies.

Prepare the mix according to the package directions and pour into the muffin or cupcake tins to two-thirds full.

Insert a Reese's peanut butter cup in the center of each cupcake. Bake 20 minutes, or until the brownie or cake tests done. No frosting necessary.

Hint: If you want a less dense cupcake, use cake mix instead of brownie mix.

Marshmallow Brownie Cupcakes

Another version of this cupcake is to use a heaping tablespoonful of marshmallow creme for the center of each cupcake. Mmmmm . . . good!

Marbled Brownies

These were very popular at Chocoholics Bakery. They are appealing and delicious.

Brownie Batter

½ cup flour
½ teaspoon baking powder
Pinch of salt
2 eggs
¾ cup sugar

1 tablespoon vanilla
4 ounces semisweet chocolate,
   melted and cooled
3 tablespoons butter
¾ cups chopped nuts

Preheat oven to 350°. Butter and flour an 8-inch baking pan. Mix together the flour, baking powder, and salt. Set aside.

Beat the eggs until thick; add sugar and vanilla. Continue to beat until very thick. Melt chocolate and butter together in the microwave.

Combine the chocolate-butter mixture and the dry ingredients. Beat well. Reserve ¾ cup of this mixture. Stir chopped nuts into the remaining batter.

Cream Cheese Marbling

4 ounces cream cheese, at room
   temperature
2 tablespoons butter, at room
   temperature

1 teaspoon vanilla
¼ cup sugar
1 egg

Use a mixer to beat the cream cheese and butter until smooth. Add vanilla and sugar and beat until fluffy.

Add the egg. Spread the cream cheese mixture over the brownies. Place heaping teaspoons of the ¾ cup brownie mix you saved from the original batter over the cream cheese mixture.

With a knife or spatula, cut through the mounds in a zigzag pattern, going almost to the bottom of the pan. Sprinkle with nuts. Bake 35 minutes. Cool completely before cutting the brownies into squares.

Peanut Butter Brownies

Follow recipe for Marbled Brownies. Add ½ cup peanut butter to the cream cheese mixture for a fabulous peanut butter brownie.

Caramel Brownies

Makes
8 1½ x 1½-inch
brownies

My friend Kathy Sikora gave me this recipe and told me that it caused havoc at a wedding because people were fighting for the brownies. Make these when you want to serve pure decadence! The hardest part is unwrapping all the caramels.

1 pound caramels, unwrapped
⅔ cup evaporated milk
1 box Swiss chocolate cake mix
1½ sticks melted butter
1 cup chopped nuts
1 package semisweet chocolate chips

Preheat the oven to 350°. Melt caramels together with ⅓ cup of evaporated milk in the top of a double boiler. Set aside to cool.

Combine the cake mix with the remaining ⅓ cup of evaporated milk, butter, and nuts. The dough will be stiff. Press half of the dough into a 9 x 13-inch baking pan that has been greased and floured. Bake 6 minutes.

Spread chocolate chips over the dough and top with the caramel-milk mix. Sprinkle the remaining dough over the top. Bake brownies an additional 15 to 18 minutes, or until golden. Cool and cut into squares.

Hint: Eliminate the caramels and evaporated milk and use half a container of apple-dipping caramel sauce, available in the produce department of large supermarkets.

Magic Foolproof Brownies

Makes
24 1½ x 3¼-
inch brownies

These are moist, easy to prepare, and virtually foolproof. If you have leftover brownies, they make terrific Rum Balls (page 195).

1 (18.25-ounce) box chocolate cake mix
1 stick butter, at room temperature
¼ cup brown sugar, tightly packed
¼ cup water
2 eggs
½ cup finely chopped nuts

Topping

1 (16-ounce) can chocolate frosting
½ cup chopped nuts

Preheat oven to 375°. Butter and flour a 9 x 13-inch baking pan. Mix together everything except topping ingredients, and beat until smooth.

Spread the batter evenly in the prepared baking pan and bake until top is firm when touched, 25 to 30 minutes. Do not overbake. Cool 15 minutes.

Run a knife around the edge of the brownies to loosen and invert onto a platter. Spread the top with frosting and sprinkle with nuts. Cut into bars.

Oatmeal Brownies

Makes
48 1½ x 1½-
inch brownies

These are chewy and perfect for backpacking. They contain no chocolate but they are still delicious. You can add nuts or raisins—or both.

1½ sticks butter, melted
1 cup brown sugar, tightly packed
¼ cup sugar
6 cups quick-cooking oatmeal
½ cup flour
2 teaspoons baking powder
2 teaspoons cinnamon
2 eggs, slightly beaten

Preheat oven to 350°. Butter and flour a 9 x 13-inch pan. Combine all the ingredients and pour into the prepared pan. Bake 15 minutes. Reduce temperature to 300° and bake an additional 25 minutes. Cool the brownies and cut into squares.

$\mathcal{S}$CRUMPTIOUS $\mathcal{C}$OOKIES

There are recipes here for traditional cookies as well as a few untraditional ones—like Potato Chip Cookies, which taste like fabulous crunchy shortbread. Have fun choosing a favorite!

Hints for Perfect Cookies

- After your cookie dough is prepared, cover the dough and chill it for at least an hour before baking the cookies.
- Prepare the batter several days in advance and chill the cookie dough well before shaping the cookies in rolls or balls. Your dough will require less flour and the cookies will be lighter in texture.
- I have been very successful at rolling cookie dough into a log and covering it with clear plastic wrap or foil and freezing the dough. When you are ready to bake the cookies, simply unwrap the dough, slice it using a serrated knife, and bake.
- It is also very easy to shape the dough into balls and then freeze it. Place frozen cookie balls on a cookie sheet and defrosting will take only a few minutes.
- Invest in a heavy cookie sheet, preferably one with sides. If you use parchment baking paper, cleanup will be a breeze. Allow the cookie sheet to cool before baking another sheet of cookies.
- Because oven temperatures vary, check each batch of cookies after 10 minutes to see if they are baked. If they are soft or appear to be shiny, continue to bake.

Biscotti

Makes
36 biscotti

This is a very old recipe. It is also remarkably simple considering that biscotti is very expensive to buy. These twice-baked cookies, also known as *Mandelbrot*, stay fresh forever—they actually get better when they are stale. These are less dry than commercial biscotti because the cookies will be fresh when you bake them. I always bake a double batch to keep in my pantry.

2 eggs
1 cup sugar
1 cup vegetable or canola oil
2½ cups flour
1 teaspoon baking soda
1 teaspoon baking powder
1 tablespoon vanilla
1 cup chopped nuts such as almonds, walnuts, pecans, or hazelnuts
1 cup chocolate chips, optional
½ cup raisins, optional
Cinnamon and sugar for dusting

Preheat oven to 300°. Cover a cookie sheet with parchment paper or spray it lightly with vegetable spray.

Mix the eggs and sugar until very thick and lemon-colored. Add the oil slowly. Add flour slowly, together with the baking soda and baking powder.

Add vanilla, nuts, and optional chocolate chips and raisins. Chill the dough for several hours or overnight.

This is a soft and sticky dough. When you are ready to bake the biscotti, shape the dough into 2 to 4 small loaves with your dampened fingers.

Since this dough spreads, don't place the loaves close together. Use 2 cookie sheets if necessary. Bake the biscotti until it is golden brown, about 30 minutes. Remove the cookie sheets from the oven and sprinkle the biscotti with a sugar-cinnamon mixture.

Cool the biscotti slightly. Use a sharp hand spatula or a knife to cut into diagonal slices. Separate the slices on the cookie sheet.

Return cookie sheets to the oven. Turn off the oven heat and leave trays in the oven overnight so the cookies can become dry—or twice-baked as they are known.

Chocolate Biscotti

Add ¼ cup sifted cocoa to the basic biscotti recipe after eggs, oil, and sugar are blended, then proceed with instructions.

Reduced-Calorie Biscotti

Replace ½ cup of the oil in the basic biscotti recipe with ½ cup of unsweetened applesauce. Omit the nuts and chocolate. Proceed with instructions.

Peanut Butter Cookies

Makes
72 cookies

What dessert cookbook is complete without peanut butter cookies? Here is my favorite recipe. Underbake them and they will be soft. Overbake them and crunch away!

1 stick butter, at room temperature
1 cup peanut butter, smooth or chunky
1 cup sugar
1 cup brown sugar, tightly packed
2 eggs, well beaten
1 teaspoon vanilla
2½ cups flour
1 teaspoon baking powder
1 teaspoon baking soda
1 teaspoon salt

Preheat oven to 350°. You will need two ungreased cookie sheets. Using a mixer, combine the butter and peanut butter and beat until very smooth. Add the sugars and beat until well mixed. Add the eggs and vanilla. Beat in the dry ingredients and mix well.

Chill dough for at least 1 hour. Shape into 1-inch balls. Place on an ungreased cookie sheet and flatten each cookie with a fork—making a criss-cross design on the tops. Bake 12 minutes, or until golden brown.

Peanut Butter Kisses

**Makes
36 cookies**

These are inexpensive to make and delicious to eat. Who could ask for anything more?

2 egg whites
Pinch of cream of tartar
⅔ cup sugar
½ cup chunky peanut butter

Preheat oven to 300° and butter a cookie sheet.

Beat egg whites until they are foamy; slowly add the sugar and beat until stiff. Fold in the peanut butter carefully. Drop by the teaspoonful onto the prepared cookie sheet. Or use a pastry tube with a large star tip and press these onto the cookie sheet.

Bake for 25 minutes, or until lightly browned.

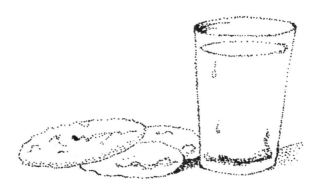

Zucchini Bars

Makes
24 1½ x 3¼-
inch bars

I live in a part of the world where zucchini grows to huge proportions. In the fall, there is usually a box of zucchini outside our little post office, free for the taking.

This is a dense, moist bar cookie that freezes very well.

1½ cups flour
¾ cup brown sugar, tightly packed
1 teaspoon baking powder
¼ teaspoon baking soda
½ teaspoon cinnamon
3 cups grated zucchini
2 eggs
¼ cup honey
1 tablespoon vanilla
½ cup vegetable or canola oil
½ cup chopped nuts

Preheat oven to 350°. Butter and lightly flour a 9 x 13-inch baking pan. Combine dry ingredients in a large mixing bowl. Stir together zucchini, eggs, honey, vanilla, and oil; add to dry ingredients. Stir until just combined.

Add chopped nuts. Pour into a greased 9 x 13-inch baking pan and bake 25 to 30 minutes. Frost with a cream cheese frosting or dust with powdered sugar. Cut into bars.

C heesecake Bars

Makes
12 squares or
24 triangles

This is an interesting way to serve cheesecake as a finger food. You can flavor them as you like: eliminate the lemon flavoring and marble the cheesecake bars with chocolate.

Crust

5 tablespoons butter
⅓ cup brown sugar, tightly packed
1 cup flour
½ cup chopped nuts

Cheesecake

½ cup sugar
1 (8-ounce) package cream cheese
1 teaspoon vanilla
2 tablespoons lemon juice, or any flavoring
1 egg
2 tablespoons milk

Preheat oven to 350°. Butter an 8-inch square baking pan and dust lightly with flour.

To make the crust, use a mixer to cream together the butter and brown sugar. Add flour and nuts. Save 1 cup of this mixture to use for topping the cheesecake bars. Press the remaining dough into the bottom of the prepared pan.

Bake the crust 15 minutes while you prepare the filling. Cream together sugar and cream cheese until smooth. Add vanilla, lemon juice, egg, and milk and beat together until there are no lumps.

Spread the cream cheese mixture over the bottom crust and sprinkle the cup of dough you saved on top of the cream cheese.

Return pan to oven and bake an additional 20 minutes. Remove from the oven and cool. Refrigerate until chilled and cut into squares or triangles.

Hint: This recipe can be doubled and baked in a 9 x 13-inch pan.

*P*otato Chip Cookies

Makes
72 cookies

This recipe is in honor of my sister Selma Eisner, who considers potato chips comfort food. They are really quite delicious. I used the Hawaiian salt-free potato chips and found them irresistible, and the cookies I made with salted chips were equally fabulous. They taste like crunchy shortbread cookies.

1 cup sugar
4 sticks butter
1 teaspoon vanilla
3½ cups flour
2 cups crushed potato chips (about 4 ounces)
1 cup chopped pecans, optional

Preheat oven to 350°. Use ungreased cookie sheets. Cream together the sugar and butter until light and fluffy. Add vanilla and flour. Add potato chips and nuts.

Place cookies together as close as you like; they do not spread. Bake 10 to 12 minutes. Remove from cookie sheets and complete cooling on paper towels. These cookies improve with time.

*G*ingerbread Cookies

Makes
36 cookies

These are easy, soft, and delicious.

1 (18.25-ounce) box spice cake mix
2 eggs
⅓ cup vegetable or oil
⅓ cup molasses
1 tablespoon ginger

Combine cake mix, eggs, oil, molasses, and ginger; stir until moistened. Refrigerate for several hours, or until the batter thickens.

Preheat oven to 350°. Roll out the dough to about ¼ inch. Use a cookie cutter and decorate as you please. You can add raisins to the batter if you like or use raisins or nuts as decorations for your gingerbread men.

If you prefer, you can form the dough into a log, slice the cookies with a serrated knife, and use a cookie press or the bottom of a drinking glass that has been moistened and dipped into sugar for a design on each cookie.

Bake 12 to 15 minutes, or until golden brown.

Hint:

To make gingerbread ornaments to hang on your Christmas tree, follow Gingerbread Cookies recipe and add ½ cup of flour to the cake mix for a stiffer batter. Be sure to make a hole in the top of each cookie before baking so that you can string a ribbon through it. Bake the cookies for 15 to 20 minutes (instead of 12 to 15), or until they are very crisp.

Danish Butter Cookies

**Makes
48 cookies**

These are delicately flavored, chewy cookies that are infinitely better than those you get for Christmas in a fancy tin—because they are freshly made by you!

4 sticks sweet butter, at room temperature
3 cups powdered sugar
3 eggs
2 teaspoons vanilla
Pinch of salt
2 teaspoons cream of tartar
2 teaspoons baking soda
5 cups flour
1 teaspoon cardamom or cinnamon

Preheat oven to 350°. Prepare two ungreased cookie sheets. Blend the butter, sugar, eggs, vanilla, and salt together until well combined. Add remaining ingredients and mix thoroughly.

Shape the dough into balls the size of a walnut and place them on the cookie sheets. Use a cookie press or the bottom of a glass moistened with water and dipped in sugar to mark the tops of each cookie.

Bake 8 minutes, or until the cookies are just turning brown. Don't overbake.

Chinese Almond Cookies

Makes
36 cookies

These cookies are almost as good as the ones you can buy in China-town.

2 cups whole almonds
1 cup flour
½ teaspoon baking powder
Pinch of salt
1 stick butter
⅓ cup sugar
1 teaspoon almond flavoring
1 tablespoon gin, vodka, or water

Set aside 36 whole almonds to decorate the cookies. Preheat oven to 350° and cover 2 cookie sheets with parchment paper.

Grind the remaining almonds using the metal blade of a food processor. Sift together flour, baking powder, and salt. Cream butter and sugar until they are light and fluffy; stir in the remaining ingredients.

Form the dough into 36 balls and place a whole almond in the center of each ball. Bake the cookies 20 minutes, or until they are golden brown.

*H*eavenly Shortbread

Makes
36 cookies

This recipe is a legacy from my beloved Bobbi LaSalle, my guardian angel.

2½ cups sifted flour
¾ cup extra-fine sugar
2 sticks butter, at room temperature
1 egg yolk
1½ teaspoons vanilla

Combine all the ingredients by hand. If you use a mixer, you will need to ball up the dough with your fingers and knead it until all the crumbs are blended. I rolled the dough forming a long coil, wrapped it in clear plastic, chilled it for a few hours, then unwrapped it. I next sliced it with a serrated knife, marked a design on top of the cookies with the bottom of a glass that had a design on its bottom, and baked the cookies. If you have a fancy cookie stamp, use it.

Preheat the oven to 300°. Reduce temperature to 250° and bake the shortbread very slowly—it might take as long as an hour, but don't let the cookies brown. Sprinkle some extra-fine sugar on the tops if you like.

*C*hocolate Shortbread

Makes
48 cookies

Adding cocoa results in a slightly drier cookie—so bake it only about 50 minutes.

2 cups flour
2 sticks sweet butter, at room temperature
¼ cup unsweetened cocoa
⅔ cup sugar

You will need one or two ungreased cookie sheets. Combine the ingredients by hand or with a mixer. Gather dough together in your hand and knead it until it is no longer crumbly. Shape into a log about 2 inches thick. Wrap and chill for at least 1 hour.

Preheat oven to 300°. Reduce oven temperature to 250°. Remove cookie dough from the refrigerator and unwrap. Using a serrated bread knife, cut the slices ⅛ to ¼ inch thick. The dough will spread only about 20 percent while baking. Place cookies in the oven and bake 50 minutes. These are lovely to serve with fresh fruit for an afternoon tea.

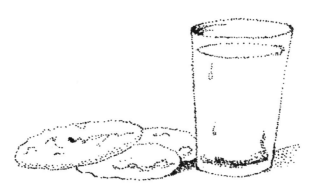

Chocolate Chip Cookies

Makes
100 small
cookies

This is my favorite chocolate chip cookie recipe. We used to bake these at least 3 inches across. You can add nuts, use any flavor of chocolate chips, chunks of chocolate, or M&Ms. They are even good overbaked because they become crisp and crunchy.

2½ cups flour
½ teaspoon baking soda
Pinch of salt
1 cup dark brown sugar, tightly packed
½ cup sugar
2 sticks butter, at room temperature
1 tablespoon vanilla
2 large eggs
12 ounces chocolate chips

Preheat oven to 325°. You will need at least 2 ungreased cookie sheets. Cover them with parchment paper if you have it.

Combine flour, baking soda, and salt and set aside. Blend the sugars in a mixer and cream with the softened butter. Scrape down the sides and bottom of the bowl. Add vanilla and eggs; mix until light and fluffy. Add the flour mixture. Do not overmix. Add chocolate chips.

Drop the dough by teaspoonfuls onto an ungreased cookie sheet 2 inches apart—these cookies spread. Bake 20 minutes, or until golden brown. Transfer cookies to a cold surface using a spatula.

Chocolate Chunk Cookies

Follow Chocolate Chip Cookie recipe and substitute 12 ounces chopped semisweet chocolate for the chips.

Chocolate Chip Cakes

I added 4 ounces of softened cream cheese to the basic recipe and the cookies became cakelike, very light and delicious.

Turtle Cookies

**Makes
48 cookies**

This is the cookie version of the popular turtle candy. Serve them in candy cups and watch the fun.

1 pound pecan halves
1 pound caramels, unwrapped
1½ sticks butter, at room temperature
1 (18.25-ounce) box Swiss chocolate cake mix
2 large eggs
1 (16-ounce) can chocolate frosting

Preheat oven to 375°. Use one or two ungreased cookie sheets. For each cookie, place 6 pecan halves on the cookie sheet to represent the head, tail, arms, and legs of the turtle.

Unwrap the caramels and flatten each one with your fingertips onto the pecan halves. Using a mixer, combine the softened butter with the cake mix and eggs, beating until smooth.

Place 1 heaping teaspoon of the batter in the center of each caramel-pecan cluster. Bake 8 to 10 minutes, or until the centers of the cookies are puffed.

Remove from the oven and cool. Microwave the can of frosting 45 seconds, or until soft. Stir frosting and pour it into a shallow bowl. Dip the top of each cookie in the chocolate and place on wax paper to dry.

*M*eringue Cookies

Makes
48 cookies

This is an excellent way to get rid of leftover egg whites. Meringue cookies are surprisingly low in fat, calories, and cholesterol. They will keep for a long time stored in an airtight container.

4 egg whites, at room temperature
Pinch of salt
1 cup extra-fine sugar
1 tablespoon vanilla

Preheat oven to 250°. Cover a cookie sheet with foil or parchment paper. Beat the egg whites until foamy and slowly add the salt and sugar. Beat until stiff, thick, and shiny. Add vanilla.

Drop the meringue by the spoonful onto the cookie sheet or use a pastry tube fitted with a large metal star tip.

Bake 30 minutes. Turn off the oven and leave meringues in the oven overnight.

Hint: If you use the pastry tube, squeeze the meringue onto the cookie sheet so that each meringue resembles a kiss.

*F*lavorful Meringues

When you add the vanilla, you can add cocoa if you want chocolate meringue cookies. Add 1 tablespoon of powdered gelatin for a change of color and taste. If you desire, add 1 cup semisweet chocolate chips or a cup of chopped nuts.

Coconut Macaroons

Makes
36 small or 12
enormous
macaroons

Macaroons were among the most popular items at Chocoholics Bakery. Most bakeries use a mix from Semper. This recipe comes close and is easy. We tubed them out using a pastry bag with a large metal star tip.

After the macaroons were baked and cooled, we dipped the bottoms in melted chocolate and drizzled chocolate over the tops. They are deliciously satisfying.

1½ cups flaked coconut
2 tablespoons flour
Pinch of salt
2 egg whites
⅓ cup extra-fine sugar
½ teaspoon almond extract

Preheat oven to 325°. Cover two cookie sheets with parchment paper or foil. Combine coconut, flour, and salt. Using a mixer, whip the egg whites in a separate bowl until they are almost stiff; add sugar and beat until the egg whites are stiff but shiny. Fold in the dry ingredients and the flavoring.

Tube onto a cookie sheet or drop by teaspoonfuls. Bake 25 to 30 minutes, or until the cookies are golden brown. Remove macaroons from the cookie sheets immediately. Cool and store in an airtight container.

*F*lorentines

Makes
24 florentines

You can roll the individual cookies around a wooden spoon handle if you do it while the cookies are still very warm. When the rolled florentines are completely cooled, fill them with flavored whipped cream, Buttercream Frosting (page 74), or Cream Cheese Frosting (page 75). Store them in an airtight container. They are incredibly delicious, delicate, and crunchy.

½ stick unsalted butter, melted
¼ cup light corn syrup
¼ cup brown sugar, tightly packed
⅓ cup flour
1 teaspoon vanilla
¼ cup finely chopped unsalted nuts

Preheat oven to 350°. Butter two cookie sheets. Melt butter over low heat; add corn syrup and brown sugar, stirring constantly until sugar is dissolved. Remove mixture from heat. Stir in flour, vanilla, and nuts.

When the batter is cool, shape it into small balls about the size of a walnut. Place cookie balls onto the prepared cookie sheet. These cookies spread, so allow 2 inches between. Press down onto each cookie ball to form a circle.

Bake florentines 5 minutes, then turn the cookie sheet around and continue to bake another 5 minutes, or until the cookies are brown. Cool cookies on the cookie sheet for a few minutes then carefully remove them using a spatula or your fingertips. If desired, curl the warm cookies around a wooden spoon handle. Complete cooling by placing the cookies on paper towels.

*C*hocolate Florentines

After cooling florentines, melt 4 ounces finely chopped semisweet chocolate, or ½ cup chocolate chips. Spread a thin layer on the bottom of each cookie. You can sandwich two cookies together, or dip the edges of each cookie in the melted chocolate.

Old-Fashioned Fruit Bars

Makes
36 cookies

These are fabulous cookie bars, a soft version of biscotti—slightly spicy and chewy. You can use any dried fruit: cranberries, cherries, strawberries, or blueberries.

¾ cup raisins
¾ cup dried fruit
2 tablespoons brandy or orange
   juice
1 cup very hot water
1 stick butter, at room
   temperature
½ cup sugar
½ cup brown sugar, tightly packed

2 eggs
1 tablespoon vanilla
1 teaspoon cinnamon
½ teaspoon baking soda
1¾ cups flour
1 cup chopped nuts
Cinnamon-sugar mixture for
   dusting

Combine the raisins, dried fruits, brandy or orange juice, and hot water; set aside to soak.

Preheat oven to 350°. Spray one cookie sheet with nonstick spray or cover the sheet with parchment paper. Use a mixer to mix together the butter, both sugars, the eggs, and vanilla. Beat until light and fluffy. Beat in the cinnamon, baking soda, and flour.

Drain the dried fruit (which has been soaking in hot water and orange juice) and add to batter along with chopped nuts.

Moisten your hands and form the dough into two long rolls on the cookie sheets. The dough will be sticky; you will have to form the rolls directly on the cookie sheet. Sprinkle the tops of the rolls generously with a mixture of cinnamon and sugar.

Bake 15 minutes, or until golden brown. Cool 15 minutes then cut the logs diagonally into ½-inch bars. Return cookie sheet to oven and bake 5 additional minutes. Turn off the heat and allow cookies to remain in the oven for several hours.

Hint: If the fruit you are using is larger than a raisin, chop the fruit using a food processor with a metal blade.

Lemon Poppy Seed Shortbread Bars

Makes
16 2 x 2-inch
bars

These are delightful. Eliminate the poppy seeds if they aren't your pleasure.

1 stick sweet butter, at room temperature
½ cup powdered sugar
1 teaspoon vanilla
1 tablespoon lemon extract or juice
2 tablespoons grated lemon zest
2 tablespoons poppy seeds
1 cup flour
Powdered sugar for dusting

Preheat oven to 350°. Butter and flour an 8-inch square baking pan. Use a mixer to cream the butter and sugar together until light and fluffy. Add vanilla, lemon juice, and zest. Add the poppy seeds and flour and beat until just mixed. Press into the bottom of the baking pan and bake at 30 to 35 minutes, or until golden. Let cool. Cut into bars. Sprinkle with powdered sugar.

Lemony Cheesecake Bars

Makes
36 1 x 2-inch
bars

Another recipe from my adorable friend Ann Leen. These are simple to prepare and delightful to serve.

1 (18.25-ounce) box lemon cake mix with pudding
2 eggs
⅓ cup vegetable or canola oil
1 (8-ounce) package cream cheese
⅓ cup sugar
1 tablespoon lemon juice or lemon extract
¼ teaspoon lemon peel

Preheat the oven to 350°. Use an ungreased 9 x 13-inch cake pan. Combine the cake mix, 1 egg, and the oil; stir until mixed. Save 1 cup of this mixture. Pat the remaining mixture into the bottom of the pan and bake 15 minutes.

Using a mixer, beat together the cream cheese, sugar, lemon juice, lemon peel, and the other egg until well mixed. Spread this mixture over the baked layer and sprinkle with the saved mixture.

Bake an additional 15 minutes. Remove pan from oven and cool completely before cutting into bars.

$\mathcal{R}$ugelach

$\mathcal{M}$akes
36 rugelach

Rugelach are nut-filled crescents that are classic Jewish treats. You will find the standard recipe and a simplified version here. The cream cheese dough in the first recipe can be used for cookies as well as turnovers or pie crust.

1 (8-ounce) package cream cheese, at room temperature
2 sticks sweet butter, at room temperature
2 cups flour
Powdered sugar
½ cup sugar
1 teaspoon cinnamon
1 cup chopped nuts
½ cup raisins, soaked and drained

Put the cream cheese, butter, and flour into a deep bowl and, using your fingers, combine the ingredients until you have a smooth dough. Form into a ball, wrap in plastic, and refrigerate at least 1 hour. (This can be prepared up to a week in advance if you prefer.)

When the dough is chilled, rub powdered sugar on your work surface. Cut dough in half and roll into a circle about ⅛ inch thick. Refrigerate the dough you are not using. Work quickly—it is difficult to use when it is not cold. Cut the circle into 16 parts, like a pie.

Combine sugar, cinnamon, nuts, and raisins. Sprinkle each wedge with the nut mixture and roll, like a tiny croissant, from the wide to the pointed edge. Refrigerate for an hour while you preheat the oven to 350°.

Bake 15 to 20 minutes, or until lightly golden. The rugelach will still be soft when you first remove them from the oven.

Easy Rugelach

Use 2 (8-ounce) packages of canned crescent rolls that you find near the dairy department at the grocery store. Follow directions on the package. Roll out individual wedges. Brush on a little melted butter before sprinkling with the raisin-nut mixture. Roll up.

Refrigerate 1 hour. Bake 15 to 20 minutes. Drizzle with a powdered sugar and milk glaze; let cool.

Hint: You can use preserves in place of the nut mixture in either recipe.

Eleven-Layer Cookie Bars

Makes
117 1-inch
squares

The recipe for these wonderful treats came from Laurie Climan, the owner of Oh! Chocolate! Bakery in Calgary, Canada. These cookies are chock full of yummies. Get the kids to help you make these because they'll be gone in a flash. Cut them into one-inch squares and pass the dessert tray.

1 stick butter, melted
1½ cups graham cracker or chocolate cookie crumbs
1 cup milk chocolate chips
1 cup semisweet chocolate chips
1 cup peanut butter chips
1 cup butterscotch chips
1 cup Heath bar chips
½ cup chopped pecans
1 cup flaked coconut
1 (14-ounce) can sweetened condensed milk
2 additional cups semisweet chocolate chips

Preheat oven to 350°. Spray a 9 x 13-inch baking pan with nonstick spray and dust lightly with flour. Pour the melted butter into the pan and spread it evenly over the bottom. Sprinkle the graham cracker crumbs evenly over the melted butter. Sprinkle the chocolate chips over the graham cracker crumbs. Cover with peanut butter chips, butterscotch chips, Heath bar chips, and pecans and spread them as evenly as possible over the chocolate chips. Spread coconut on top of everything and drizzle the sweetened condensed milk over all.

Press down on the mixture with your fingertips. Bake 25 minutes, or until the cake is golden brown.

Remove from oven and cool 15 minutes. Melt the additional 2 cups of chocolate chips in the microwave and spread it over the cooled cake. Sprinkle with additional chopped nuts if desired. Cut the cake into 1-inch squares when completely cooled.

Mexican Wedding Cake Cookies

Makes
100 bite-sized
cookies

These cookies were my daughter Lisa's favorite cookies when she was little. Shape them into bite-sized morsels and serve them in small candy cups.

¾ cup powdered sugar
½ teaspoon cinnamon
2 sticks butter, cut into small pieces
1 teaspoon vanilla
Pinch of salt
1 cup chopped pecans, optional
2 cups flour
Powdered sugar for dusting

Preheat oven to 350° and cover two cookie trays with parchment paper. Using a food processor, combine all ingredients except flour and process until the butter and sugar are blended. Mix in the flour.

Shape into bite-sized morsels. Bake 20 minutes, or until they are firm. Remove cookies from the oven and roll them in powdered sugar while they are still hot.

After cookies are cooled, you may want to roll them in powdered sugar a second time.

*W*hite Chocolate Chunk Cookies

Makes
48 cookies

These can be soft and chewy or crisp and crunchy. Just increase the baking time to make them crisp.

2 sticks butter, at room temperature
½ cup sugar
1 cup brown sugar, tightly packed
2 large eggs
1 tablespoon vanilla
1½ cups flour
1 teaspoon baking soda
Pinch of salt
¾ pound fine white chocolate broken into chunks

Preheat oven to 300°. Spray two cookie sheets lightly with nonstick spray. Cream together butter and sugars until light and fluffy. Add eggs and vanilla. Add dry ingredients and mix until smooth. Add the chopped white chocolate.

Drop by tablespoonfuls onto the prepared cookie sheets and bake 20 minutes, or until the cookies are golden brown.

Hint: Use 2 cups of white chocolate chips instead of the chopped white chocolate.

Oatmeal Crisp Cookies

Makes
60 cookies

Thanks for this recipe go to Lolita Leen. These cookies are crunchy and keep very well.

1 cup brown sugar, tightly packed
1 cup sugar
2 sticks butter, at room temperature
2 large eggs
1 teaspoon vanilla
1½ cups flour
Pinch of salt
1 teaspoon baking soda
3 cups quick oatmeal
1 cup chopped walnuts

Cream the sugars and butter together. Add eggs and vanilla. Add dry ingredients, adding oatmeal and walnuts last.

Form dough into small balls about the size of a walnut and chill for an hour. If you prefer, form the dough into long rolls, wrap in clear plastic, and chill. Unwrap the roll of dough and slice ¼ inch thick.

Bake 10 minutes, or until golden brown.

Hint: If you want a spicier cookie, add 1 teaspoon cinnamon.

$\mathcal{S}$UBLIME $\mathcal{P}$IES

$\mathcal{I}$t seems like every region in America boasts its own special variety of pie—from apple to pecan to key lime, to name just a few. The sheer variety can drive a pie-lover into a delicious quandary: how can you possibly choose between a dense, rich chocolate concoction, a fresh fruit tart, and a light and airy meringue?

Apart from favorite fillings, everyone seems to have a special recipe for the perfect crust. At the end of this chapter you'll find several recipes for piecrusts to complement all types of fillings. If, however, you have a craving for pie, are pressed for time, and just can't wait, don't hesitate to pick up a crust from the refrigerated case at the supermarket. It may not be quite as perfect as a homemade crust, but it is a delicious shortcut.

Mississippi Mud Pie

**Serves
8 to 12**

A fast and easy dessert to make and one that everyone loves.

1 quart coffee ice cream
1 cup caramel or butterscotch topping
1 cup fudge sauce
1 (9-inch) chocolate cookie crust

Spoon ice cream into the prepared crust and press the ice cream down into the crust. Freeze for 15 minutes. Spoon caramel or butterscotch sauce on top of the ice cream and return pie to the freezer. Spoon hot fudge sauce over the top of the entire pie. Freeze pie until serving time. (This can be stored for at least a month.) Remove the pie from the freezer 15 to 30 minutes before serving. Decorate the top with whipped cream or whipped topping.

Boston Cream Pie

Serves
8 to 12

This is really a cake but has been called a pie for as long as it has been in existence. There is a luscious layer of cream filling between two layers of spongy yellow cake topped off with a chocolate glazed frosting.

It's very simple. Bake a yellow cake mix using the Magic Cake Mix recipe (page 20). Pour batter into a buttered 9-inch springform pan. Freeze the cake after it has been baked, cooled, and removed from the pan.

Boston Cream Filling

½ cup sugar
¼ cup flour
1½ cups light cream
4 egg yolks
1 teaspoon vanilla

Grated rind of 1 orange
1 teaspoon orange juice or
    orange flavoring
1 cup heavy cream

Use a heavy saucepan. Combine sugar and flour. Stir in the light cream and cook over medium heat until thickened.

Remove mixture from heat. Beat egg yolks in a small bowl. Stir a little of the hot mixture into the yolks and pour this into the sugar-flour-cream mixture. (This way the egg yolks will not curdle.)

Cook 2 more minutes. Stir in vanilla, orange rind, and orange juice. Cool. Whip the heavy cream and fold into the egg mixture. Refrigerate.

Split the frozen cake layer in half and fill the center with the cream filling. Drizzle chocolate glaze or frosting over the top.

Easy Boston Cream Pie

Serves
12

1 (9-inch) yellow cake (see Magic Cake Mix, page 20)
1 (3.4-ounce) box vanilla instant pudding
1 tablespoon orange juice or extract
1 cup whipping cream

Bake cake according to Magic Cake Mix recipe and let cool. Freeze and split in half. Prepare instant pudding according to package directions. Whip cream until stiff; fold pudding mix, orange flavoring, and whipped cream together. Chill and use as filling between the cake layers. Microwave a can of prepared frosting and use as a glaze. Refrigerate until served.

French Silk Pie

**Serves
8**

This is a no-bake pie. Buy or make a 9-inch graham cracker, cookie, or chocolate crust.

1 stick butter, at room temperature
¾ cup extra-fine sugar
4 tablespoons cocoa
3 extra large eggs, at room temperature

Cream butter, sugar, and cocoa until very well mixed. Scrape the bowl so there are no lumps in the batter. Add eggs, one at a time, and beat for several minutes after the addition of each egg to get air into your filling.

Scrape down the bowl frequently. Pour filling into the prepared crust and refrigerate. This dessert can be served at room temperature, refrigerated, or frozen—but store it in the refrigerator before serving.

Decorate the top of the pie with whipped cream and chocolate curls.

Hint: If you don't have time to warm the eggs to room temperature, soak them in warm water for 5 minutes first.

*B*lack Russian Pie

Serves
8

You can make this in your food processor; it is easy and impressive. Because this pie is unbaked, it is quite simple to prepare.

½ cup milk
2 envelopes unflavored gelatin
½ cup Kahlua
⅓ cup vodka
2 eggs
½ cup sugar
1½ cups whipped cream
1 (8-inch) prepared graham cracker or chocolate piecrust.

Chill the pie crust for 10 minutes. Heat milk to boiling and remove from heat. Add gelatin and stir until dissolved. Cool 10 minutes then stir in the Kahlua and vodka.

Use a food processor or blender to mix the eggs and sugar. With the machine running, pour in the milk and gelatin mixture. Fold in whipped cream; blend well.

Transfer to a bowl and chill until thickened, 15 to 30 minutes. Stir occasionally. Chill until set, about 3 hours. Spoon the filling into the prepared crust. Decorate the pie with shaved chocolate and serve with joy!

Osh-A-Pie

**Serves
12**

This one is for those who love meringue. It's a takeoff of the Pavlova cake from Australia. I've named it in honor of my granddaughter, Ocea Skyhorse, because they are both equally sweet.

Meringue Shell

4 egg whites
¼ teaspoon cream of tartar
1 cup sugar

Preheat oven to 300°. Beat egg whites with cream of tartar until foamy. Add sugar, a little at a time, and continue to beat until egg whites are stiff and glossy. Spread meringue into a 10-inch pie pan, making a deep ridge at the edges. Bake 1 hour and cool.

Filling

4 eggs, separated
8 ounces semisweet chocolate, melted and cooled
1 tablespoon vanilla
1½ cups whipped cream

Beat egg yolks until they are thick and lemon-colored (reserve whites). Fold chocolate into the egg yolks. Add vanilla.

Beat egg whites until stiff and fold them carefully into the chocolate mixture. Fold half the whipped cream into chocolate mixture and pour it into the meringue shell.

Decorate pie with the remaining whipped cream. Chill until firm, about 4 hours.

Coconut Cream Pie

Serves
8

Here's an old-fashioned pie sure to delight coconut lovers.

1 (14-ounce) can sweetened condensed milk
1 (3.4-ounce) package regular, not instant, pudding
4 egg yolks
½ cup water
8 ounces sour cream
½ cup lightly toasted coconut
Whipped cream or whipped topping
1 (8-inch) prepared piecrust

Combine condensed milk, pudding mix, egg yolks, and water in the top of a double boiler over boiling water. Stir until the mixture is thick. Remove from heat and cool.

When mixture is at room temperature, stir in sour cream and all but a handful of toasted coconut. Pour mixture into the prepared crust and refrigerate until firm.

Top with whipped cream and sprinkle with toasted coconut.

Chocolate Meringue Pie

Serves
8

Creamy and delicious, this is one of those times when using pudding mix just won't do.

3 tablespoons cornstarch
Pinch of salt
1¼ cups sugar
2 cups light cream
2 squares unsweetened chocolate, chopped
2 eggs, separated
1 tablespoon butter
1 teaspoon vanilla
1 (8-inch) prepared piecrust

In a saucepan, mix together cornstarch, salt, and 1 cup of the sugar. Gradually add light cream. Add chopped chocolate; stir until mixture comes to a boil and becomes thick. Stir and cook 1 more minute. Remove pan from heat.

Stir in egg yolks (reserve whites for the meringue), adding a little of the hot mixture to the yolks before adding the yolks to the hot mixture. Cook and stir 1 minute. Stir in butter and vanilla.

Remove mixture from heat and cool 15 minutes. Using a whisk, beat the chocolate mixture until it is smooth; pour it into the prepared crust. Refrigerate the pie while you prepare the meringue.

Preheat oven to 425°. To prepare the meringue, beat egg whites until foamy; add the remaining ¼ cup sugar and beat until stiff.

Spread meringue over the top of the pie and bake in a hot oven 5 to 7 minutes, or until the meringue is golden brown. Refrigerate the pie when it is completely cooled.

Hint: To prevent the meringue from weeping or falling, spread meringue on top of pie after the chocolate has cooled to room temperature.

Chocolate Banana Cream Pie

Follow recipe for Chocolate Meringue Pie. Add sliced bananas and presto: a chocolate banana cream pie!

Key Lime Pie

Serves 8

One of America's most treasured pies, key lime pie is very easy to prepare. If you use individual pie pans, pile the meringue on high and sprinkle with flaked coconut.

½ cup lime juice
1 can sweetened condensed milk
2 tablespoons grated lime peel
4 eggs, separated
½ teaspoon cream of tartar
⅓ cup sugar
1 (8-inch) prepared piecrust

Preheat oven to 350°. Combine lime juice, sweetened condensed milk, lime peel, and the egg yolks (reserve whites); stir until smooth. Pour mixture into the prepared crust.

Beat egg whites until foamy; add cream of tartar and sugar and beat until stiff. Spread the meringue on top of the pie and bake 15 minutes, or until the meringue is golden. Refrigerate until served.

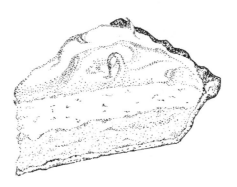

Kahlua Pie

Serves 12

This was rated the number one dessert at Chocoholics Dessert Parlor. It can be eaten frozen, at room temperature, or refrigerated. Use a prepared chocolate cookie crumb crust if you prefer, but here is how to make it yourself.

Chocolate Crumb Crust

1½ cups flour
1 stick butter, at room temperature
¼ cup firmly packed brown sugar
¾ cup chopped pecans
1 ounce grated unsweetened chocolate
1 teaspoon vanilla
1 tablespoon water

Preheat oven to 350°. Combine all ingredients and blend well. Butter a 10-inch pie pan; press the mixture onto the sides and bottom of the pan using your moistened fingertips. Bake crust 10 minutes, or until brown.

Filling

1½ sticks butter at room temperature
1 cup extra-fine sugar
1½ ounces unsweetened chocolate, melted and cooled
1 tablespoon instant coffee
3 eggs

Beat butter until very creamy. Add sugar and continue beating until light and fluffy. Add chocolate and instant coffee and beat well. Add eggs, one at a time, beating well after each addition. Mix on high until the mixture is very thick and fluffy. Pour filling into the cooled pie shell and refrigerate, covered, for at least 12 hours.

Topping

2 cups whipping cream
½ cup powdered sugar
2 tablespoons instant coffee
2 tablespoons Kahlua, or any coffee-flavored liqueur
Chocolate curls or chocolate coffee beans for garnish

Whip the cream until almost stiff. Add powdered sugar, coffee, and liqueur. Spread or pipe the cream over the filling using a pastry tube so that the whipped cream topping is very high. Garnish with chocolate curls or chocolate coffee beans. Refrigerate several hours, or freeze for as long as 6 weeks. Serve frozen or defrosted.

Strawberry Chiffon Pie

Serves
8

Start out with a baked crust and create this summer treat. Garnish with fresh strawberries and serve with whipped topping or whipped cream.

1 (3.4-ounce) package strawberry gelatin
1 cup boiling water
½ cup lemon-lime soda or ginger ale
1 (10-ounce) package frozen sliced strawberries
1 quart fresh strawberries
1 (16-ounce) container whipped topping
1 (9-inch) prepared piecrust

Dissolve gelatin in boiling water and add soda. Stir until gelatin is dissolved; stir in frozen sliced strawberries.

Refrigerate gelatin until it is almost set. Add 1 cup of whipped topping and mix until smooth. Pour into the prepared crust and decorate with fresh strawberries.

Chill pie until it is firm; garnish with remaining whipped topping.

Hint: You can substitute any flavor of gelatin in the recipe for Strawberry Chiffon Pie. Try watermelon-flavored gelatin and decorated the top of the pie with chunks of seedless watermelon. It's fantastic!

Lemon Meringue Pie

Serves 8

I thought that my lemon pie was the best ever—until I tried Ann Landers' recipe. She claims to have received it from a New York cab driver. If you have lemon curd available, you may use it for lemon pie filling—it is simple and delicious.

1¼ cups sugar
6 tablespoons cornstarch
3 eggs, separated
⅓ cup lemon juice
2 cups water

3 tablespoons butter
2 teaspoons white vinegar
1 tablespoon lemon extract
1 (9-inch) baked piecrust

Use the top of a double boiler. Mix together the sugar and cornstarch. Beat together the egg yolks and lemon juice; add this mixture to the sugar mixture together with the water. Cook over boiling water for 25 minutes, or until thickened. Add butter, vinegar, and lemon extract and stir the mixture thoroughly.

Pour into prepared pie crust and let cool. Prepare the meringue.

Meringue

1 tablespoon cornstarch
2 tablespoons cold water
½ cup boiling water
1 teaspoon vanilla

Pinch of salt
3 egg whites
6 tablespoons sugar

Blend cornstarch and cold water in a saucepan. Add hot water; cook until the syrup is clear and thickened. Allow mixture to cool completely. Add vanilla and salt.

Preheat oven to 400°. In a separate bowl, beat egg whites until they are foamy; gradually add sugar and beat until stiff but not dry. Add the cornstarch mixture and beat well.

Spread meringue over the cooled pie filling and bake 10 minutes, or until the meringue is browned.

Liqueur Pie

Graham cracker crust

These pies made with liqueur are delightful to serve. Use the basic recipe and change the liqueur flavors to suit your taste.

1 envelope unflavored gelatin
½ cup cold water
4 eggs, separated
Pinch of salt
⅔ cup sugar
½ cup liqueur (see variations below)
1 cup whipped cream
1 (9-inch) prepared vanilla, chocolate, or graham cracker piecrust

Pour gelatin and water into a saucepan and stir until mixed. Add egg yolks, salt, ⅓ cup sugar, and liqueur; mix together. Heat on low until gelatin dissolves, stirring constantly, until the mixture thickens. Don't let this mixture come to a boil. Beat egg whites until almost stiff and add the remaining ⅓ cup sugar. Beat until stiff.

Fold meringue into the cooled, thickened egg-sugar mixture. Fold whipped cream into this mixture and pour into the prepared crust.

Refrigerate the pie for 6 hours or more. Garnish with fresh fruit or additional whipped cream piped into rosettes and serve.

Galliano Pie

Use the Liqueur Pie recipe, substituting the following for the liqueur and water:

¼ cup Galliano
¼ cup Cointreau
¾ cup orange juice (instead of the water)
2 teaspoons grated orange peel

Grasshopper Pie

Use Liqueur Pie recipe, substituting the following for the liqueur:

¼ cup white creme de menthe
¼ cup green creme de menthe
Chocolate cookie crust

Brandy Alexander Pie

Use Liqueur Pie recipe, substituting the following for the liqueur:

¼ cup cognac
¼ cup creme de cocoa
Graham cracker crust
Chocolate curls for garnish

Easy Pecan Pie

**Serves
8 to 12**

Easy and very delicious. Use your favorite unbaked piecrust.

3 eggs, slightly beaten
1 cup dark corn syrup
1 cup sugar
Pinch of salt
2 tablespoons melted butter
1 teaspoon vanilla
1 cup pecans
1 (10-inch) prepared piecrust

Preheat oven to 400°. Prepare an unbaked crust for a 10-inch pie pan; set aside while you prepare the filling.

Combine all the ingredients and stir until smooth. Pour mixture into the unbaked crust. Bake 15 minutes. Lower oven temperature to 350° and bake an additional 35 minutes, or until a knife comes out clean when inserted in the center of the pie.

Chocolate Pecan Pie

Follow instructions for Easy Pecan Pie. Add to batter 2 ounces of melted and cooled bittersweet or semisweet chocolate, or 4 tablespoons cocoa and 1 tablespoon melted butter.

Nut Raisin Pie

Serves
8 to 12

If you love raisins and nuts, this pie is for you. It is a heavy dessert—
perfect after a light dinner. It is quite sweet, reminiscent of mincemeat
without the lard.

3 eggs
¾ cup dark corn syrup
⅓ cup firmly packed brown sugar
½ stick butter, melted
1 teaspoon vanilla
Pinch of salt
1 cup raisins
1 cup chopped pecans
1 (9-inch) unbaked piecrust

Preheat oven to 350°. Beat eggs until thick and lemon-colored. Stir in
corn syrup and brown sugar, melted butter, vanilla, and salt. Stir in
raisins and nuts and pour mixture into the prepared crust.

Bake 40 to 50 minutes, or until a knife inserted in the center of the
pie comes out clean. Remove from oven and cool. Serve with vanilla ice
cream or whipped topping.

Sweet Potato Pie

Serves 12

Similar in taste and texture to pumpkin pie, this is fun to serve. You will need a baked pie crust in either a 10-inch tart pan with a removable bottom or a 10-inch pie pan.

3 cups cooked yams or sweet potatoes, fresh or canned
¾ cup whipping cream
½ cup milk
½ cup sugar
3 eggs, slightly beaten
⅓ cup plus 1 tablespoon bourbon
1 tablespoon butter, melted
1 teaspoon cinnamon
Pinch of salt
½ cup brown sugar, tightly packed
¾ stick butter, at room temperature
2 tablespoons ginger
½ cup chopped pecans
18 pecan halves

Preheat oven to 350° and prepare the crust. Bake piecrust and set aside to cool.

Using a mixer, combine the cooked sweet potatoes, cream, milk, sugar, eggs, ⅓ cup bourbon, melted butter, cinnamon, and salt. Beat until well blended and pour into the baked crust.

Bake 50 minutes, or until a knife inserted in the center of the pie comes out clean. Cool to room temperature.

Combine the brown sugar, ¾ stick butter, ginger, and 1 tablespoon bourbon; stir until well mixed. Stir in chopped pecans and spoon evenly over the top of the pie. Arrange pecan halves around the edges of the pie.

Place pie on an ungreased cookie sheet 6 to 8 inches under a hot broiler. Cover the edges of the crust with foil to prevent burning. Broil for a minute or two, or until the topping is bubbling. Cool to room temperature and refrigerate until served.

Pumpkin Chiffon Pie

Serves
8 to 12

This is a very old recipe that was given to me when I was young. It is a marvelous pie. You can substitute canned cooked sweet potatoes or yams for the pumpkin.

1¼ cups canned pumpkin, mashed
Pinch of salt
½ cup brown sugar, tightly packed
3 egg yolks
1 teaspoon cinnamon
¼ teaspoon ginger
¼ teaspoon nutmeg
1 package unflavored gelatin
¼ cup cold water
3 egg whites
½ cup sugar
1 cup whipping cream
2 tablespoons powdered sugar
1 (8-inch) prepared piecrust

In a saucepan, combine pumpkin, salt, brown sugar, egg yolks, and spices. Cook 5 minutes until well blended.

Dissolve gelatin in cold water and stir into the hot pumpkin mixture. Refrigerate 30 minutes.

Beat egg whites until foamy. Add sugar and beat until stiff. Fold egg whites into the cooled pumpkin mixture and mound into the prepared piecrust.

Beat whipping cream until frothy. Add powdered sugar and beat until stiff. Pile on top of the pumpkin mixture. Sprinkle with cinnamon. Refrigerate several hours and serve.

Dessert Pizza

**Serves
12 to 18**

Thanks for this recipe go to Ann Leen. You can use the sugar cookie dough that you find in the frozen food section or make your own. The Heavenly Shortbread recipe (page 122) works well for the crust. This is a stunning and easy dessert for which you will receive applause and fame.

1 (20-ounce) package slice-and-bake sugar cookies
⅓ cup sugar
1 (8-ounce) package cream cheese, at room temperature
3 tablespoons brandy or liqueur
½ teaspoon vanilla
4 cups thinly sliced fruit (such as kiwi, strawberries, blackberries, bananas)
½ cup apricot preserves without chunks

Preheat oven to 375°. Cover a large pizza pan with foil. Cut the cookie dough into rounds and press onto the pizza pan so that the pan is completely covered. Prick the dough with a fork. Bake until dough is golden, about 10 minutes. Cool completely.

Combine sugar, cream cheese, liqueur, and vanilla using a mixer; beat until smooth. Spread evenly over the cookie crust.

Arrange the fruit in a circular pattern over the cream cheese—use your imagination and design abilities. Melt the apricot jam in your microwave, adding a little water if necessary. Brush jam over the fruit. This will serve as a preservative to keep the fruit from turning dark. Cover and let chill for an hour.

Butterscotch Chocolate Pie

Serves
8

Who could ask for anything more? This is a very old recipe given to me by one of my customers. I made it for him and he ate the entire pie in one sitting!

⅓ cup flour
¾ cup tightly packed brown sugar
Pinch of salt
2½ cups light cream
2 egg yolks, well beaten
6 tablespoons chocolate syrup or fudge sauce
1 teaspoon vanilla
2 tablespoons butter
1 (8-inch) prepared piecrust

In a saucepan, combine flour, brown sugar, and salt; mix in cream and beaten egg yolks. Cook until mixture is thickened, stirring constantly. Add the chocolate sauce or syrup.

Remove from heat and add vanilla and butter. Pour into prepared crust and refrigerate until set. Decorate with whipped cream.

*P*iecrust

Truthfully, I am a proponent of baking the easiest way and often use the boxed crusts purchased in the dairy department at the supermarket. However, if you prefer to do it yourself, here are some recipes, all of which can be prepared in a food processor.

*B*utter Piecrust

Makes
2 crusts

2 cups flour
1 teaspoon salt
1 stick butter, cut into small pieces
⅓ cup cold water

Use the metal blade in the food processor. Combine all the ingredients except the water and process until particles resemble coarse crumbs— about 20 seconds.

Add water all at once and process until the dough forms a ball, about 30 seconds. Shape the ball with your hands and chill 30 minutes. Roll out the dough to fit the pie pan.

If the pie filling is to be added after the crust is baked, bake the crust at 400° until golden brown, about 15 minutes. Be sure to prick the dough all over with the tip of a fork so the dough will not puff.

*O*ld-Fashioned Piecrust

Use the directions for Butter Piecrust, but substitute ½ cup lard for the butter, cut into small pieces, and add an additional tablespoonful of water.

*S*tandard Piecrust

Use directions for Butter Piecrust, but substitute vegetable shortening, cut into pieces at room temperature, for the butter.

Perfect Piecrust

Makes
2 crusts
(9-inch)

My son-in-law Loren is a great cook. This is the piecrust he makes and it is, like him, perfect.

3 cups flour
1 teaspoon salt
1⅓ cups good quality vegetable shortening
1 small egg
1 teaspoon vinegar
¼ cup cold water

Combine flour and salt and cut in the shortening. Put half the mixture into your hands and squeeze so mixture is just barely holding together. If it is too moist, add a little flour. If it's too dry, add a little shortening.

Beat the egg together with the vinegar and 2 tablespoons of cold water; add to the flour mixture. Stir to blend. Add remaining water, one tablespoon at a time, until dough is a little sticky but not gooey.

Divide dough in half and form it into two large balls. Place one ball between two sheets of wax paper and flatten slightly. Roll out the dough in short, shaping movements until it is a circle 12 inches in diameter.

Place the dough into a 9-inch pie pan so the dough overlaps the pan. Remove wax paper.

If you are making a single piecrust, use half of the dough, crimp the pie edges, prick dough all over with the tines of a fork, and bake at 400° until it is golden brown, about 15 minutes.

If your pie has a top and bottom crust, repeat rolling out the top layer of crust. Fill the pie before baking and press the top crust onto the bottom crust and crimp the edges. Cut 3 slits into the top piecrust to allow it to breathe. Brush the top of the pie with melted butter and sprinkle some sugar on top before baking.

Graham Cracker Crumb Piecrust

Makes
1 crust
(10-inch)

This recipe is enough to line a 10-inch springform pan if you are making cheesecake, or a 10-inch pie pan.

1½ cups graham cracker crumbs
¼ cup sugar
½ teaspoon cinnamon
1 stick butter, melted

Combine all ingredients and press into the bottom and sides of a greased springform or pie pan. If you want a crunchy crust, bake in a preheated oven at 350° for 10 minutes.

Hint: You can replace the graham crackers with vanilla wafers or chocolate cookies. Make crumbs using a food processor.

Chocolate Coconut Piecrust

Makes
1 crust
(9-inch)

This crust is easy to prepare because it is unbaked. It is also the perfect base for cream pies.

½ cup semisweet chocolate chips
¼ stick butter
2 cups coconut, flaked

Butter a 9-inch pie pan; set aside. Melt chocolate chips and butter together in microwave. Allow chocolate to cool a few minutes. Stir in coconut and immediately scrape into the prepared pie pan; spread mixture to cover the sides and bottom of the pan.

Chocolate Nut Piecrust

Makes
1 crust
(9-inch)

This unbaked crust is a wonderful foundation for the Kahlua Pie—and any cream pie you choose to make.

1 cup chopped nuts, any kind
¼ cup semisweet chocolate chips
¼ stick butter, cut into chunks
2 tablespoons milk
¾ cup powdered sugar

Toast the nuts in microwave by spreading them in an ungreased glass baking dish or on paper towels. Cook nuts 5 minutes on high. Remove from microwave. Cool and chop nuts into small bits. (You can use a food processor to do this but only turn the motor on for a few seconds at a time or you'll have nut butter.)

Combine the chocolate chips, butter, and milk in a large Pyrex measuring cup and heat in the microwave until the chocolate and butter are melted. Stir until the mixture is well blended.

Stir in powdered sugar and chopped, toasted nuts. Press into the bottom and sides of a 9-inch pie pan. Refrigerate until set. Fill with your favorite filling.

GLORIOUS FUDGE, CANDIES, AND NUTS

Nearly everyone admits to having a sweet tooth that needs to be satisfied (some of us more often than others). Whether your favorite treat is rich chocolate, gooey caramel, candied nuts, or luscious fudge, you're sure to find something in this chapter to please your palate.

You may be surprised to see how easy your favorite confections are to make. Within this chapter are the time-saving secrets for creating chocolate truffles, caramel pecan turtles, chocolate creams, marzipan, and many more little luxuries.

Many of these candies make great gifts. Place the treats in a decorative tin, pretty glass jar, or other elegant container tied with a colorful ribbon, and everyone will be thrilled to receive your homemade gourmet confections.

Best of all, even diabetics can enjoy sweets by substituting ⅔ cup of fructose for each 1 cup of sugar in recipes.

Chocolate Truffles

Makes
18 large
24 small

Nobody knows the truffles I've seen, but this is an easy recipe. All you need is an adventurous spirit and cold hands. If your hands are always warm, pat your hands with a cloth soaked in ice water.

This is also known as ganache and is sensational used as filling and frosting for a cake or torte.

Basic Ganache

8 ounces fine semisweet chocolate, broken into small pieces
1 cup whipping cream, at room temperature
Melted chocolate and sweetened cocoa for dipping

Melt chocolate and cream together and mix until they are combined well. Pour mixture into a small bowl and chill several hours, or even several days, covered.

Shape ganache into small balls using a scoop or a spoon. Handle as little as possible and remember to keep those fingers cold.

Refrigerate until you are ready to dip the truffles in melted chocolate or roll in sweetened cocoa. *Do not refrigerate* the truffles after they have been dipped in chocolate, or they will get sticky or have white streaks. Keep them in a cool place at about 65° to 70°. Or, they can be frozen successfully and thawed.

You can also pour the ganache into a baking pan, chill it until firm, cut it into squares, and dip it in melted chocolate. Use a fondue fork to lift the squares out of the chocolate. Drop onto waxed paper and dry.

Food Processor Truffles

Makes
36

12 ounces semisweet chocolate chips
¼ cup whipping cream
¼ cup Kahlua

Use a food processor with metal blade and chop the chips until fine. Combine the Kahlua and cream in an 8-cup Pyrex measuring cup with a handle; microwave the mixture until it boils.

    With the motor of the food processor on, pour in the hot cream mixture until the chocolate is completely melted. Pour the mixture into small candy cups. Refrigerate until set.

Hint: You can replace the Kahlua with any liqueur you prefer or you can use vanilla. If you use Kahlua, garnish each truffle with a coffee bean, real or candied, on the top.

*C*hocolate *W*alnut *F*udge

Makes
36 squares

Easy, delicious, and almost foolproof.

12 ounces semisweet chocolate chips
1 can sweetened condensed milk
2 cups mini marshmallows
1 tablespoon vanilla
1 cup chopped nuts

Melt chocolate chips, condensed milk, and marshmallows together in a large saucepan, stirring constantly. When the mixture is very smooth and thickened, add vanilla and chopped nuts. Pour the fudge into a buttered 8-inch square pan. Chill fudge, cut it into squares, and enjoy.

Chocolate Pecan Balls

Makes
60 small
pecan balls

These are simple to make and quite impressive to serve. Eliminate the cocoa and they are still delicious. Let the kids help make these. They resemble Mexican Wedding Cake cookies and are easiest to eat if they are bite-sized.

2½ sticks butter, at room temperature
1 cup powdered sugar
½ cup cocoa
2 cups flour
1 tablespoon vanilla
1½ cups chopped pecans

Preheat oven to 350°. Lightly spray a cookie sheet with nonstick spray.

Cream butter and sugar together until they are well blended. Add cocoa, flour, vanilla, and pecans. Chill for at least 1 hour.

Shape dough into small balls, about the size of a large marble. Bake 30 minutes. Remove from oven. When cool enough to handle, roll in additional powdered sugar.

Momma Rita's Easy Fudge

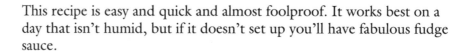

Makes
2½ pounds

This recipe is easy and quick and almost foolproof. It works best on a day that isn't humid, but if it doesn't set up you'll have fabulous fudge sauce.

1 (5-ounce) can evaporated milk
2¼ cups sugar
1 stick butter, at room temperature
1 tablespoon vanilla
1½ cups chopped nuts
12 ounces chocolate chips
6 ounces milk chocolate chips

Use a microwavable bowl that holds at least 12 cups. Mix the evaporated milk and sugar together. Microwave for 3 minutes. Stir and microwave another 3 minutes, until mixture reaches a full boil. Microwave an additional 2 minutes, until sugar is well dissolved and the mixture is foamy.

Place the remaining ingredients in a large bowl. Pour the boiling mixture over these ingredients, and stir until very well mixed. Pour into a buttered 8-inch square pan, let cool, and enjoy!

Fudge Balls

Makes
72 fudge balls

Fudge Balls were my granddaughter Ocea's all-time favorite candy. Make a batch of Momma Rita's Easy Fudge. After the fudge is cooled, cut it into squares then work the fudge into a round ball.

Melt 2 cups of milk chocolate chips in the top of a double boiler, or use artificial chocolate coating and melt it in the microwave. Dip the individual fudge balls. Set on wax paper to dry and decorate each fudge ball with a walnut half.

Chocolate Bark

**Makes
2 pounds**

Making Chocolate Bark provides almost instant gratification because it is fast and easy. This should be fun for kids to make.

6 ounces semisweet, milk chocolate, or white chocolate chips, or 1 cup
   of each
6 ounces milk chocolate chips
1 tablespoon vegetable oil
1 cup chopped nuts
6 ounces white chocolate, optional
½ cup raisins, optional

Line a cookie sheet with aluminum foil. Melt the chocolate chips and oil together in the top of a double boiler. Stir the chocolate until it is smooth. Cool for 10 minutes. Stir nuts and optional white chocolate into the melted chocolate.
   Add optional raisins and pour the mixture onto the cookie sheet. Use a spatula to spread the chocolate to a thickness of about ¼ inch.
   Refrigerate 20 to 30 minutes until set and break into chunks.

White Chocolate Bark

Replace the semisweet and milk chocolate with white chocolate; melt in the top of a double boiler over hot but not boiling water.

Chocolate Candy Clusters

Use the recipe for Chocolate Bark and add mini marshmallows or peanut butter chips. Drop mixture onto waxed paper by the spoonful.

Easy Chocolate Creams

Makes
36

These elegant creams can be dipped in melted chocolate for a dessert tray. You will amaze your guests.

8 ounces semisweet chocolate
1 cup powdered sugar
1 tablespoon cream
1 egg, well beaten
½ cup chocolate sprinkles or sweetened cocoa

Melt chocolate in the microwave, stirring occasionally until melted. Quickly stir in the powdered sugar, cream, and egg.

Refrigerate until the mixture is hard enough to shape into small balls about the size of truffles. Roll the mixture into small balls and roll in chocolate sprinkles or cocoa. Place the individual candies in pretty candy cups.

Hint: If you want to dip these in chocolate, refrigerate the balls while you are preparing the melted chocolate.

Chocolate Mint Patties

Makes
about 5 dozen

These are lovely to serve after dinner with coffee. They are very easy to make. Spoon the mixture directly into foil candy cups or drop the mixture by the teaspoonful.

½ stick butter
3 tablespoons cream
1 (13.25-ounce) package chocolate fudge frosting mix
1 teaspoon peppermint extract

Using the top of a double boiler, combine butter and cream until melted. Add frosting mix and cook 15 minutes, or until thickened. Stir in peppermint flavoring.

Spoon 1 teaspoon of mixture into paper cups or drop onto wax paper; make a swirl design on the top of each candy with your spoon or your fingertip.

Hint: If the mixture thickens too fast, add a little hot water and stir.

Peanut Butter Fudge

**Makes
64
1-inch squares**

This is a very simple recipe. Try using filbert butter or cashew butter instead of peanut butter.

½ stick butter
2 cups sugar
½ cup milk
4 tablespoons marshmallow creme
1 teaspoon vanilla
1 cup peanut butter

Place butter, sugar, and milk into a heavy saucepan and bring the mixture to a boil. Cook for 3 minutes. Remove pot from heat and stir in marshmallow creme, vanilla, and peanut butter.

Pour the mixture into a buttered 8-inch square pan and cool.

Hint: This is easier to cut into 1-inch squares just before it is hard.

English Toffee

Makes
2 pounds

This candy is so marvelous, you should consider making a double batch. It's easier to make if you choose a dry day; humidity in the air will make this difficult to prepare.

1¼ cups light brown sugar, firmly packed
¼ cup corn syrup
5 tablespoons sweet butter, cut into small chunks
1 tablespoon cider vinegar
¼ cup water
1 teaspoon vanilla
1 cup semisweet chocolate chips, melted
¾ cup chopped, roasted, and salted cashews, pecans, or walnuts

Butter a cookie sheet with sides and set aside. In a heavy 2-quart saucepan, combine sugar, corn syrup, butter, vinegar, and water. Bring mixture to a full boil. Stir until sugar is dissolved. Boil syrup over medium heat until it reaches 290° on a candy thermometer.

Stir in vanilla. Pour mixture onto the prepared pan. Spread using a wooden spoon and allow to harden.

When the toffee is hard, melt chocolate chips in a microwave and spread chocolate over the toffee. Sprinkle nuts over the chocolate, and press them into the toffee.

When the toffee is cool, break it into pieces. Store in an airtight container.

Caramel Pecan Turtles

Makes
36 large or 60
small turtles

At Chocoholics Bakery we made these very large with each turtle weighing half a pound. You can experiment with the size of your creations.

3 cups pecan halves
2 cups light brown sugar, tightly packed
1 cup sugar
Pinch of salt
1 cup heavy cream
¼ teaspoon cream of tartar
1 stick butter, cut into small bits
1 tablespoon vanilla
8 ounces semisweet chocolate

Oil two large cookie sheets. Toast pecans for 10 minutes in an oven heated to 325°.

Use a heavy 2-quart saucepan. Combine the sugars, salt, cream, and cream of tartar. Cook until the mixture reaches 238° on a candy thermometer. Use a wet brush to wash down any sugar crystals that form on the side of the pan.

Remove pan from heat and allow the mixture to cool to 220°. Add butter chunks and vanilla. Beat mixture until creamy and add pecans. Working quickly, drop the mixture by heaping tablespoonfuls onto the greased cookie sheets and allow to cool.

When the candies are hard, brush the tops with melted semisweet chocolate. Wrap the pieces in clear wrap and store in an airtight container.

Easy Caramel Pecan Turtles

1 pound pecans
1 pound caramels, unwrapped
8 ounces semisweet chocolate

Preheat oven to 325°. Spread 1 pound of pecans on an ungreased cookie sheet and toast the nuts for 10 minutes. Cool completely before using.

Place six pecans in a cluster, one for the head, one for the tail, and two each for the arms and legs of the turtle. Press a softened caramel onto the pecans. Brush the tops of the pieces with melted semisweet chocolate. Wrap the turtles individually in clear wrap, and store in an airtight container.

Melt-In-Your-Mouth Toffee

Makes
2 pounds

This candy is not only crunchy and delicious, it actually melts in your mouth. Choose a dry, warm day to make this, or it might be sticky.

1 cup sugar
Pinch of salt
¼ cup water
1 stick butter
1 cup chopped nuts
1 cup chocolate chips, melted

Butter a cookie sheet. In a heavy saucepan, combine the sugar, salt, water, and butter. Cook until the mixture reaches the soft crack stage, 270° on a candy thermometer.

Stir in ½ cup of the nuts and pour immediately onto the prepared cookie sheet. Use a spatula to spread the candy out to about ¼ inch thick. Allow candy to cool completely.

Melt chocolate chips in the microwave and spread on top of the toffee. Sprinkle the remaining ½ cup nuts on top of the chocolate before the chocolate hardens.

When the candy is completely cool, break it into pieces and send me some!

Microwave Caramels

Makes
2 pounds

Caramel is a great addition to lots of cakes and cheesecakes. It's also divine over ice cream.

I live in an area where the humidity is always close to 100 percent. It is best to make caramels on a very warm and dry day. If this recipe doesn't harden, use your imagination—or a big spoon!

3 sticks butter, at room temperature
2 cups extra-fine sugar
1½ cups light corn syrup
1 (12-ounce) can evaporated milk
1 tablespoon vanilla
1 cup chopped nuts, optional

Use an 8-cup Pyrex measuring cup with a handle or a 2-quart glass bowl to melt the butter in the microwave. Add sugar, corn syrup, and half of the milk; mix together.

Cook in the microwave for about 20 minutes, turning the bowl every 5 minutes and stirring with a wooden spoon. Add the remaining milk and stir the mixture. Return bowl to microwave and cook an additional 8 to 10 minutes, or until the mixture has reached the soft ball stage, 234° on a candy thermometer.

Add vanilla and nuts; beat by hand for 1 minute. Pour into a buttered 9 x 13-inch pan and cool for 3 hours.

Cut into squares and wrap each piece in wax paper. Or use the batch to create special delights like caramel pecan turtles.

Peanut Brittle

Makes about 2 pounds

Karen Koog gave me this recipe years ago and told me that it was former President Jimmy Carter's favorite. True or not, here it is. The big secrets are to be very fast when you are pouring the mixture into the pans and to spread the candy as thin as possible using a spatula.

1 cup sugar
1½ cups water
1 cup corn syrup
3 cups raw peanuts
1 tablespoon baking soda
1 stick softened butter
1 tablespoon vanilla

Use a heavy 3-quart saucepan. Stir together sugar, water, and corn syrup. Stir constantly, using medium-high heat, until the mixture comes to a boil and reaches 232° on a candy thermometer.

Stir in the peanuts. Continue boiling; stir frequently until the mixture reaches 300°.

Remove from heat and stir in the baking soda, butter, and vanilla. *Quickly* pour onto two lightly oiled cookie sheets and spread it as thin as possible using a spatula. Allow the candy to cool completely before breaking it into pieces.

Peanut Butter Candy Treats

Makes
117 1-inch
squares

This easy candy recipe is great on a dessert tray or for gift giving. Place each 1-inch square in a paper candy cup for a lovely presentation.

24 graham crackers, crushed
2 sticks butter, melted
1 cup peanut butter
4 cups powdered sugar
12 ounces chocolate chips, melted and cooled

Combine graham cracker crumbs with melted butter, peanut butter, and powdered sugar and press into the bottom of a buttered 9 x 13-inch pan. Refrigerate until firm.

Melt chocolate chips in your microwave and pour over the graham cracker mixture. Spread the chocolate to completely cover. Cut into 1-inch squares before refrigerating.

Oh! Nuts!

Makes
1¼ pounds

This recipe came to me thanks to my lifelong friend, Betty Lias. The result is very professional despite the fact that it is easy to make. These are just like those candied pecans that cost $20 a pound. You will astound yourself.

1 pound of pecans, almonds, walnuts, or hazelnuts
2 egg whites
1 cup sugar
Pinch of salt
1 teaspoon cinnamon, optional
1 stick butter, melted

Preheat oven to 325°. Spread nuts on a cookie sheet; bake 10 minutes, or until toasted. Pour the nuts onto another cookie sheet covered with several layers of paper towels.

While the nuts are cooling, beat egg whites until stiff and fold in sugar, salt, and optional cinnamon. Melt butter in a microwave and brush it evenly over the bottom of a cookie sheet.

Mix the nuts into the egg mixture and stir until the nuts are completely coated. Pour nuts onto the cookie sheet with the melted butter and stir until nuts are coated with the butter. Separate the nuts as much as possible.

Place the cookie tray in the oven and bake 30 minutes, stirring every 10 minutes and separating the nuts. Make sure the nuts are completely covered with butter.

When the nuts are done, they will look dark and crunchy. Pour them onto the cookie sheet covered with paper towels to absorb any excess butter. When the nuts are completely cool, store them in an airtight container.

Hint: These will keep for a long time. Put them in a fancy tin and they make a fabulous gift.

Gingered Meringue Nuts

Follow the Oh! Nuts! recipe and add 1 teaspoon of ginger in place of the cinnamon.

Hot and Spicy Nuts

I made the Oh! Nuts! recipe hot and spicy by reducing the sugar to ½ cup and adding ½ teaspoon chili powder, ½ teaspoon cayenne, 1 teaspoon garlic powder, a pinch of salt, 1 tablespoon soy sauce, and 1 tablespoon Worcestershire sauce. If you want these tongue-burning hot, increase the cayenne.

Sweet and Spicy Nuts

Makes
2 pounds

Another recipe thanks to Betty Lias. This time the butter is eliminated. The result is a nut with a thinner crust than the recipe for Oh! Nuts!— but equally delicious. If you like, add a teaspoon of orange flavoring for an additional taste treat.

2 cups nuts (pecans, walnuts, hazelnuts)
1 egg white
½ cup sugar
1 teaspoon cinnamon
1 teaspoon vanilla, or any flavoring

Preheat oven to 325°. Spread the nuts on a cookie sheet and toast them for 10 minutes, or until they are golden brown. Remove them from the oven and pour them onto a cookie sheet covered with several thicknesses of paper towels.

Beat egg white until stiff and add sugar, cinnamon, and flavoring. Stir the nuts into the meringue until they are well coated and spread them on the cookie sheet, separating them as much as possible.

Bake at 300° for 40 minutes, turning the nuts every 10 minutes and separating them. Remove the nuts from the oven when they appear to be crunchy, and cool on paper towels.

Store in a jar with a tightly fitting lid. Tie a ribbon around the neck of the jar and you have a lovely hostess gift.

Ginger Teriyaki Nuts

Makes
1½ pounds

This is a great snack for a cocktail party. You can use any raw nuts you like. Almonds work well in this recipe.

2 cups blanched almonds
½ stick butter, melted
3 tablespoons soy sauce
3 tablespoons dry sherry
¼ teaspoon ground ginger
Garlic salt to taste

Spread nuts on an ungreased cookie sheet that has sides. Toast the nuts in a preheated oven at 325° for 10 minutes. Pour the hot nuts on a cookie sheet covered with several layers of paper towels to cool.

When nuts have cooled, return them to the ungreased cookie sheet and spread them over the pan. Combine the melted butter, the soy sauce, sherry, and ginger. Pour over the nuts and stir to make sure they are coated on all sides.

Bake nuts for 30 minutes, turning with a spatula every 10 minutes to make sure they are evenly toasted. Spread nuts out on the cookie sheet covered with paper towels to dry. Store in a tightly capped jar.

Oven-Baked Caramel Corn with Nuts

Makes
5 quarts

This is an exciting recipe because everyone loves caramel corn and you can make this in your oven—no more burned fingers using syrup. Break this up and it resembles the expensive snack you buy. Be sure to store it in an airtight container after it has cooled.

5 quarts popped popcorn
2 cups salted peanuts, cashews, or pecans
1 cup butter
2 cups dark brown sugar, tightly packed
½ cup light corn syrup
Pinch of salt, optional

Combine the popped corn and nuts in a large baking pan and place in a preheated oven at 250°. Combine butter, brown sugar, and corn syrup in a heavy saucepan. A pinch of salt will accentuate the sweetness.

Cook and stir until the sugar dissolves. Bring mixture to a boil; cook until very thick and at the firm ball stage (a drop of syrup in a glass of water will form a firm ball), 260° on a candy thermometer.

Remove popcorn from the oven and pour the syrup over the corn and nuts. Mix well. Return popcorn to the oven and bake an additional 30 minutes. Stir every 10 minutes.

Remove popcorn from oven and spread it on wax paper to cool, breaking it into small chunks.

When completely cooled, store the caramel corn in an airtight container.

Applettes

**Makes
36**

Applettes are somewhat like gummy bears in texture but a great deal more healthful. Kids will gobble these up and consider you a genius.

Powdered sugar for dusting
1⅓ cups applesauce
3 packets unflavored gelatin
1 teaspoon cinnamon
2 cups sugar
¼ teaspoon lemon juice
1 cup chopped walnuts
1 teaspoon vanilla

Generously dust an 8-inch square glass baking dish with powdered sugar.

Mix ⅔ cup of the applesauce with the gelatin and let the combination stand for 10 minutes. Add the remaining applesauce, cinnamon, and sugar and cook over low heat for 5 minutes. Remove mixture from heat and add lemon juice, nuts, and vanilla.

Stir with a wooden spoon until the mixture is well blended. Pour mixture into the prepared pan and chill until set. Cut into squares.

Cotlettes

Substitute apricot sauce for the applesauce and follow the directions for making Applettes.

Cherry Cordials

**Makes
36**

I'll admit that this isn't an easy recipe, but it will give you great pride to announce that you made these. Please read the recipe carefully before you begin.

2 cups sugar
1 tablespoon corn syrup
¾ cup water
Pinch of salt
1 teaspoon vanilla
1 (16-ounce) jar maraschino cherries with stems
Chocolate for dipping

You need either a marble surface to work on or a cookie sheet that has been chilled in the refrigerator for several hours.

In a saucepan, combine sugar, corn syrup, water, and salt; bring to a boil, stirring constantly. Lower heat. Cover the pan and cook an additional 3 minutes. Remove cover and continue to cook the mixture without stirring until it has reached the soft ball stage, 240° on a candy thermometer.

Remove mixture from heat, add vanilla, and pour it onto a marble surface or cooled cookie sheet. Do not stir until just the center of the fondant remains slightly warm. Scrape the fondant from the center to the edge of the surface using a spatula. Work until it is stiff.

When the fondant loses its gloss and becomes crumbly, knead it with your hands until it becomes smooth and soft. The heat from your hands will allow you to knead what at first seems impossible. Wrap the fondant in plastic and refrigerate for at least 24 hours.

After the fondant has been prepared, drain a jar of cherries using a strainer. Place cherries on dry paper towels and allow to dry for at least an hour.

Melt the fondant in the top of a double boiler over simmering hot water. It will become liquid. Dip the cherries, one at a time, into the fondant and place them on wax paper to dry. Dip the cherries twice if you want a larger finished candy.

When the fondant is completely set, dip the cherries, holding them by the stem, into melted chocolate. Place the cherries on wax paper to dry completely. Store cherries in a cool, dry place—but not in the refrigerator—for a few days until the centers become liquefied.

Hint: Find a shop that sells Wilton candy-making supplies and buy their fondant mixture. It's almost foolproof and the easy fondant will liquefy in a few days just like the difficult recipe I gave you.

Crystallized Flowers

These are glorious on top of cakes, and if you use edible flowers like roses, violets, and nasturtiums, you can eat the whole flowers.

My friend Nan Marie Wineinger, who is an artist, taught me how to do this. Nan takes the flowers apart petal by petal, then reassembles the flowers on the cake. Her flowers are exquisite. Picture these crystallized flowers on top of a wedding cake! Depending on the size of the flower used, this will coat 3 to 4 flowers.

1 egg white
1 tablespoon cold water
1 cup extra-fine sugar

Mix egg white and water together until just blended. Use a paintbrush with a small, flat painting surface. Coat flower, front and back, with the egg wash.

Hold the flower over a large bowl and sprinkle with sugar, covering the entire flower. Set flower on a paper towel to dry overnight. If you are not going to use the flowers immediately, wrap them in plastic and freeze them. They will stay frozen for up to 6 weeks.

Fruity Bon Bons

Makes
about 3 dozen

These are fabulous. The only cooking required is melting the chocolate. Or roll in powdered sugar instead of chocolate.

¼ pound German baking chocolate or milk chocolate
1 cup chunky peanut butter
1 cup powdered sugar
½ cup coconut
1 cup pitted, chopped dates
½ cup finely chopped nuts
Additional melted chocolate for dipping

Melt chocolate in the top of a double boiler over simmering hot water. Remove from heat and cool.

Mix chocolate together with remaining ingredients and shape into 1-inch balls. Drop balls into melted chocolate and use a fondue fork to remove them. Shake off excess chocolate by tapping the fork against the side of the bowl; lay candies on wax paper to harden.

Hint: Refrigeration may cause the chocolate to streak and get whitish. If you roll in powdered sugar instead of chocolate, you can refrigerate these goodies.

Marzipan

Makes
2 pounds

Marzipan is simply a combination of ground almonds, sugar, and egg whites. Those who love it sometimes have a hard time finding it in stores. Here's my recipe.

1 pound blanched almonds, ground
1 pound powdered sugar, sifted
1 large egg white

Grind almonds using your food processor until they are fine. Add sugar and egg white to form a paste. Wrap marzipan in wax paper and store in the refrigerator until you need it.

Hint: This can be used between the layers of a cake, or even rolled out to cover the sides and top of the cake. It will become hard and can be frosted with a thin coating of royal icing. This makes a magnificent wedding cake but, I warn you, it is very difficult to cut and quite sweet.

Chocolate Marzipan

Makes
1½ pounds

¼ pound almond paste
1 egg white
2 cups powdered sugar, sifted or strained
2 tablespoons unsweetened cocoa
Chocolate for dipping

Use a mixer to combine almond paste and egg white. Beat until smooth. Beat in half of the powdered sugar and place the mixture on a surface lightly dusted with powdered sugar. Knead the dough while adding the remaining powdered sugar and cocoa.

Pat into a buttered 8-inch square baking pan and refrigerate until chilled, then cut into 48 squares and dip them in melted chocolate. Or, shape these into balls about the size of a truffle, refrigerate until solid, and then dip in chocolate.

Candied Orange Peels

Prepare the orange peel at least a day before you dip the tips in choco-late. I understand this recipe can be made with grapefruit peels as well.

2 oranges
Water to cover
½ cup corn syrup
1 cup extra-fine sugar
1 cup water
Sugar and chocolate for dipping

Mark the peel of the orange into eight sections. Remove peel from the orange.

In a saucepan, combine the orange peel with enough water to cover and heat to boiling. Drain water from the orange peels and repeat this process two more times. This removes the bitterness of the rind. Gently scrape off the white part of the peels with a sharp paring knife and cut the peels into narrow strips.

In a saucepan, combine the corn syrup, 1 cup sugar, and 1 cup water; heat, stirring constantly, until sugar is dissolved. Add the orange strips and bring mixture to a boil. Reduce heat and simmer gently for an hour.

Drain the liquid and place the orange strips in sugar. Mix gently and arrange on a cookie sheet. Let the orange rinds dry for at least a day before dipping the ends in melted chocolate.

Bourbon Balls

Makes
36

These candies are simple to prepare and they look wonderful on a dessert tray. You can replace the bourbon with apple juice or orange juice if you like.

1 (12-ounce) box vanilla wafers, crushed into crumbs
1 cup powdered sugar, plus some for rolling
2 tablespoons cocoa
3 tablespoons white corn syrup
¼ cup bourbon or liqueur of your choice

Mix all the ingredients together. Form into small round balls and roll in additional powdered sugar. Easy!

*R*um Balls

Makes
48

Rum balls are considered a great treat. Most bakeries use stale cake and cookies to create these delicacies. They are always just a bit different depending on the cake, muffins, cookies, or bread you use.

1 pound stale cake, or 1 (8-inch) chocolate cake layer
½ can chocolate frosting
2 tablespoons rum or rum flavoring

Mix the ingredients together. You may need to add a little more frosting to make the dough pliable.

Refrigerate for 1 hour or up to several days, covered. Shape the dough into small balls and place them on waxed paper. Refrigerate them while you prepare the chocolate coating.

Chocolate Coating

Try to find a candy-making supply store from which you can buy dipping chocolate. The best product to use for home candy making is chocolate without cocoa butter. It is artificially flavored chocolate but it is difficult to tell the difference when using it for coating candy. If you use real chocolate you will need to temper it and that can be painstakingly difficult.

1 pound Chocolate A'peels, semisweet or milk chocolate, melted

If you are melting semisweet chocolate or A'peels you can use a microwave. Place the chocolate in an 8-cup Pyrex measuring cup. Heat chocolate for 2 minutes. Remove chocolate and stir until it is smooth.

If you are melting real milk chocolate, you will have to use a double boiler.

Dip rum balls into the slightly cooled, melted chocolate. Use a toothpick, bamboo skewer, or fondue fork to hold the rum ball while dipping. Or drop the rum balls directly into the melted chocolate and remove the balls using a fondue fork.

Set the dipped candies on wax paper and allow to harden at room temperature.

Hint: Using a wooden spoon to stir chocolate will eliminate a metallic spoon taste in your candy.

Microwave Divinity

Makes
1½ pounds

Divinity is another of those goodies that is difficult to make when the humidity is high. Choose a warm, dry day and, if divinity is your delight, try this recipe.

The hardest part is measuring the corn syrup. If you spray the measuring cup with a vegetable spray before adding the corn syrup you will find it is easy to remove the syrup from the cup.

2 cups extra-fine sugar
½ cup corn syrup
⅓ cup water
2 egg whites
1 teaspoon vanilla
1½ cups chopped pecans

Using a 2-quart glass measuring cup with a handle, combine the sugar, corn syrup, and water. Microwave on high for 5 minutes. Stir until sugar is completely dissolved. Microwave another 5 minutes, or until the mixture reaches a temperature of 250° on a candy thermometer.

Use a large mixer bowl to beat the egg whites until stiff. Slowly pour the hot syrup into the egg whites using the low speed on your mixer. Continue beating mixture for 10 to 12 minutes, or until the mixture is no longer shiny.

Add vanilla, blend in pecans, and quickly press the batter into a buttered 8-inch square glass cake pan. Cool completely before cutting the divinity into squares.

DELECTABLE PASTRIES

There's something so soul satisfying about the scent of baked goods wafting from the kitchen. And one of life's greatest pleasures is biting into a warm muffin or scone slathered with butter, or pulling apart a hot glazed donut or fritter sprinkled with powdered sugar. Whether served for breakfast, brunch, or a snack with coffee or tea, pastries are a treat enjoyed by all ages.

Muffins are ideal for popping into lunch bags or taking along to work for a morning coffee break. For those of you who love giant muffins but don't have a large tin, here's a helpful tip: thoroughly clean several empty tuna cans, line them with large paper cups, fill with batter, and bake as usual.

The following recipes were popular items at Chocoholics Bakery and include many of my personal favorites.

Healthy Bran Muffins

Makes
24 regular-size,
12 huge

These muffins are unique: you can keep the batter refrigerated for at least a month and bake them fresh whenever you want them.

2 cups All-Bran cereal
1 cup Bran Buds cereal
1 cup boiling water
2 cups buttermilk
2 teaspoons baking soda
1 cup honey
2 eggs, beaten
½ cup oil
2 cups bran
1 cup flour, all purpose or whole wheat
Pinch of salt
Raisins, chopped dates, chopped nuts, optional

Preheat oven to 350°. Mix cereals together with the hot water; allow the water to be absorbed into the cereal.

Combine buttermilk, baking soda, honey, eggs, oil, and cereal mixture. Add bran, flour, and salt to the wet ingredients; mix until well blended. If you are using raisins, dates or nuts, add them now.

Pour batter into muffin tins lined with paper muffin cups, two-thirds full. Bake 20 minutes, or until muffins test done. These are fabulous served warm.

Hint: Baked in a loaf pan, this makes excellent bran bread. Slice muffins or bread into thin slices and serve as a snack.

Prune Muffins

Soak 1 cup pitted prunes in hot water for 15 minutes. Drain the prunes and run them through a food processor for a minute, until they are puréed. (Or use a cup of baby food prunes.) Add purée to the batter for a fabulous prune-bran treat.

Blueberry Muffins

Makes
12

The batter will turn blue if you refrigerate it for more than an hour, which makes for an interesting muffin color. Place the blueberries in a plastic bag with a few tablespoons of flour, shake the bag, coat the berries with flour and they will not stain your batter. You can also replace the blueberries with any fruit that you like.

½ cup sugar
½ stick butter, melted
1 egg
1¼ cups flour
2 teaspoons baking powder
Pinch of salt
½ cup milk
1 cup fresh berries or canned blueberries, drained

Preheat oven to 400°. Line your muffin tins with paper cups or use clean tuna cans lined with paper cups for huge muffins.

Cream sugar and butter together and add the egg. Mix flour, baking powder, and salt and add alternately to wet ingredients with the milk. Carefully fold in the berries.

Spoon batter into prepared muffin tins about two-thirds full. Bake 20 minutes, or until golden brown. These muffins freeze very well.

Butterscotch Orange Muffins

Makes
12

This recipe makes equally fabulous orange bread. The muffins are good enough to replace cupcakes any day.

Butterscotch Topping

1 cup butterscotch chips
1 tablespoon butter
½ cup flour

Melt butterscotch chips and butter together in the top of a double boiler or in a saucepan. Stir in the flour to make a crumbly mixture. Set aside until the muffins are ready to bake.

Orange Muffins

1½ cups flour
½ cup sugar
2 tablespoons baking powder
½ teaspoon salt
½ teaspoon cinnamon
½ cup milk
¼ cup vegetable oil
1 egg, well beaten
1 teaspoon orange flavoring
1 cup finely chopped fresh orange, peeled and seeded
1 cup butterscotch chips

Preheat oven to 375°. Prepare a muffin tin by lining the cups with paper fillers. Combine the dry ingredients and add milk, oil, egg, orange flavoring, orange chunks, and butterscotch chips. Stir until just moistened. Fill the muffin cups two-thirds full with batter and top with butterscotch topping. Bake 20 to 25 minutes, or until the muffins test dry.

*C*hocolate Pecan Muffins

Makes
12

These are very moist, heavy, and yummy.

6 ounces semisweet chocolate
3 tablespoons butter
1 cup flour
2 tablespoons sugar
2 teaspoons baking powder
½ teaspoon cinnamon
1 egg
⅓ cup buttermilk
1 teaspoon vanilla
¾ cup chopped pecans
1 cup semisweet chocolate chips

Preheat oven to 375°. Prepare a muffin tin; line the cups with paper cups.

Use the microwave to melt 6 ounces of semisweet chocolate and butter together; stir until smooth.

Combine the dry ingredients; add the egg, buttermilk, vanilla, and chocolate mixture. Stir to moisten; add chopped pecans and chocolate chips.

Fill the muffin tin three-quarters full; bake 20 to 25 minutes, or until the muffins test done.

Special Chocolate Pecan Muffins

If you have time and want very special muffins, sprinkle the following mixture on the tops before baking them:

½ cup flour
¼ cup brown sugar, tightly packed
½ teaspoon cinnamon
2 tablespoons melted butter
¼ cup chopped pecans

Cranberry Scones

Makes
8

These are a great breakfast or brunch treat. You can prepare the dough the night before and bake them in the morning. Scones are fairly dry and should be served as soon as they come out of the oven.

2 cups flour
1½ teaspoons baking powder
½ teaspoon baking soda
⅓ cup sugar
Pinch of salt
¾ stick cold butter
1 large egg
½ cup buttermilk
1 tablespoon vanilla
1 cup dried cranberries, soaked and drained

Preheat oven to 350°. No need to grease your cookie sheet.

In a large bowl, stir together the flour, baking powder, baking soda, sugar, and salt. Cut the butter into tiny cubes and add to the flour mixture. If you have a pastry knife, cut the butter into the dry ingredients until the mixture looks like coarse crumbs. This can also be prepared in a food processor using the metal blade.

Add egg, buttermilk, and vanilla to the dry ingredients; stir until just mixed.

Stir in the cranberries. Flour your hands and knead the dough for a minute or two, until the dough is smooth. Place the ball of dough onto an ungreased cookie sheet, forming a circle about ¼ inch thick. Mark the circle into 8 pie-shaped wedges.

Bake 18 to 20 minutes, or until golden brown. Cool 5 minutes. Cut into wedges and serve warm.

Hint: There are lots of scone mixes available commercially. Avoid those mixes where you need to add more than water because it is easy to put together your own ingredients. Even if you use the mix, the dough still requires a little kneading.

Currant Scones

**Makes
8**

Scones need to be baked and eaten as soon as possible after being removed from the oven—they become increasingly dry with each passing moment.

You can replace the currants (tiny raisins) with larger raisins, dates, chopped prunes, figs—your choice. I used dried blueberries and they were marvelous.

½ cup currants, soaked and drained
2 cups flour
¼ cup sugar
2 teaspoons baking powder
⅓ cup cold butter, cut into small pieces
½ cup heavy cream
1 egg
1 tablespoon vanilla or lemon flavoring
1 egg, beaten with 1 teaspoon water for glaze

First, soak dried fruit in very hot water for 15 minutes to puff them up.

Preheat oven to 425°. Lightly oil a cookie sheet or cover it with parchment paper.

Stir together the dry ingredients and cut the butter into the mix using a food processor with a metal blade. The butter-flour mixture will resemble small beans. Add ½ cup heavy cream, the egg, and flavoring. Drain the fruit and add it to the batter.

Form dough into a ball and work with your fingers until it is relatively smooth and no longer crumbly. Shape dough into a circle about 8 inches across on the cookie sheet. You can use your fingers to pat out the dough if you don't want to roll it out.

Mark the dough into 8 pie-shaped wedges. Brush egg glaze over dough. Bake 12 to 15 minutes, or until golden brown. Using a sharp knife, cut through the markings and serve as individual scones.

Fudge Waffles

**Makes
6**

We served these at the dessert parlor topped with ice cream and hot fudge sauce—delicious!

2 ounces unsweetened chocolate
½ stick butter
3 eggs
⅔ cup sugar
1 teaspoon vanilla
1 cup buttermilk
1¼ cups flour
½ teaspoon baking soda
½ teaspoon baking powder
Pinch of salt
3 ounces semisweet chocolate, chopped

Prepare the waffle maker according to directions for the machine. Melt the unsweetened chocolate and butter together in the microwave; stir until smooth. Cool. Beat eggs, sugar, and vanilla together; blend in buttermilk. Add dry ingredients; stir until smooth. Fold in chopped chocolate and bake in the waffle maker.

French Toast Soufflé

Serves
8 to 12

Oh, this is fabulously delicious. Another comfort food! This can make you famous for your brunches. You'll need an egg bread known as challah. It's even better if the bread is stale.

This can be partially prepared the night before and kept refrigerated until morning. Put it in the oven before your shower and it will be ready to serve when the coffee is brewed.

1 loaf challah bread cut into thick slices
1 stick melted butter
4 large eggs
¼ cup sugar
2 cups cream or half-and-half
1 teaspoon cinnamon
1 teaspoon vanilla
Maple syrup or jam or jelly

Preheat oven to 350°. Place the sliced egg bread in a buttered baking dish. Pour the melted butter over the bread. Mix together the eggs and sugar. Add the cream and cinnamon and vanilla.

Pour it over the bread and let it soak for at least 1 hour, or keep refrigerated overnight. Turn the slices very carefully once or twice to make sure the bread is soaked.

Try not to break the bread—it will still be delicious, only not quite as pretty. Use a pancake turner.

If the bread has been refrigerated overnight, remove it from the refrigerator and let it come to room temperature while the oven is heating to 350°.

Bake uncovered for 45 minutes or until the bread is puffy and golden brown. Serve hot.

Dinner Rolls

Serves
6

This dough can be used to bake dinner rolls and cinnamon rolls—and it's great for coffee cakes.

1 (¼-ounce) package instant yeast
1 cup warm water
3 eggs
3 tablespoons sugar
1 teaspoon salt
1 stick cold butter
4 cups flour

Dissolve the yeast in warm water; wait 5 minutes. Using a mixer, beat the eggs until thick and lemon colored. Add sugar to eggs along with the dissolved yeast and salt. Stir until just combined. Cut the cold butter into small pieces and stir into egg mixture.

Stir in flour until well combined. Cover the bowl with plastic wrap and place in a draft-free place for 2 hours, or until the dough rises.

Shape dough into dinner rolls or cinnamon-pecan rolls.

Place the shaped dough into a greased pan for sweet rolls or a greased cookie sheet for dinner rolls. Cover with a clean towel and let rise 1 hour.

Bake in a preheated oven at 350° until lightly browned.

Sweet Rolls

If you are making sweet rolls, allow the rolls to cool slightly after baking. Heat a can of vanilla frosting in the microwave for 30 seconds, then drizzle the frosting over the rolls.

Coffee Cake

Cream together one 8-ounce package of cream cheese, add 1 table-spoon of lemon juice, 1 tablespoon of grated lemon peel, and ¼ cup sugar. Use as filling for coffee cake.

To make a coffee cake ring, roll out dough into a rectangle, spread melted butter, cinnamon, chopped nuts, raisins, chopped apples—your choice of any or all of the above—roll into a long roll, shape into a ring, and bake until golden.

Cake Donuts

This is a somewhat simpler version of donuts. You'll still need a deep fryer but less patience than the raised donuts.

2½ tablespoons butter, at room temperature
¾ cup sugar
2 eggs
3 to 4 cups flour
3 teaspoons baking powder
½ teaspoon salt
1 cup milk

Mix together the butter, sugar, and eggs; combine dry ingredients. Add milk and dry ingredients, one cup at a time, until the dough is firm but not dry. Roll out the dough on a floured board and cut with a donut cutter.

Fry in hot oil, at 375°, turning the donuts once to brown both sides. Drain donuts on paper towels. Frost or leave plain.

Raised Donuts

Makes
12

If you have time and want to experiment, here's a great donut recipe. They are fried in deep, hot fat—the best!

1 cup milk
¾ cup sugar
Pinch of salt
⅓ cup shortening
1 (¼-ounce) envelope dry yeast
4 eggs
4 to 5 cups flour

Prepare a deep-fat fryer. Scald milk; stir into combined sugar, salt, and shortening. Cool to lukewarm; stir in yeast and let the mixture rest for 5 minutes.

Stir in eggs and add 4 cups of flour, one cup at a time. The dough will be thick but sticky. Knead in the remaining flour until the dough is firm but not dry.

Return dough to bowl, cover it, and allow it to rise to double in bulk. Then roll out the dough to a thickness of ⅔ inch. Cut the dough using a donut cutter and place donuts on a lightly greased cookie sheet. Cover donuts and allow them to rise again.

When the dough has risen, fry the donuts in hot oil, 375°. Turn each donut once to brown both sides. Remove donuts from oil when browned and drain on paper towels. Dip donuts in powdered sugar, or frost with your favorite frosting and sprinkle with nuts.

Lemon Blueberry Poppy Seed Bread

Serves
8 to 12

This is a quick and easy bread. It's very moist and can almost serve as a dessert. It's perfect with fruit salad on a warm summer evening.

1 teaspoon grated lemon peel
3 tablespoons lemon juice, or 1 tablespoon lemon extract
¾ cup water
2 tablespoons poppy seeds
1 package blueberry muffin mix
1 egg

Freeze a lemon for 15 minutes. Using a grater, scrape off the yellow part of the rind. Squeeze the lemon and save the juice.

Preheat oven to 350°. Spray a loaf pan with nonstick spray and dust lightly with flour.

Soak poppy seeds in water; let stand for a few minutes. Combine the muffin mix, egg, water-poppy seeds mixture, and lemon juice until moistened but not smooth. Fold in lemon peel and blueberries if they came in a separate can in the package.

Pour into prepared pan; bake 1 hour, or until cake tests done. Remove bread from the oven. Cool 15 minutes in pan and invert it onto a serving plate. Dust lightly with powdered sugar.

Hint: Use this batter for muffins.

Pumpkin Applesauce Bread

Makes
2 loaves

The invention of bread machines has lots of folks creating breads of all types. My children, Daniel and Toni, gave me their bread machine, which they never used. I have never used it.

Making bread in loaf pans is very simple. Here is the easiest recipe of all. The result is always heartwarmingly delicious.

1 (18.25-ounce) package spice cake mix
3 eggs
⅔ cup apple juice
1 cup applesauce
1 teaspoon cinnamon
1 cup canned pumpkin, mashed
1 cup chopped nuts
½ cup raisins, soaked and drained, optional

Preheat oven to 350°. Lightly spray two loaf pans with vegetable spray and dust lightly with flour; use your sugar shaker filled with flour.

Using a mixer, blend together the cake mix, eggs, and apple juice. Blend in applesauce, cinnamon, and mashed pumpkin. Stir in nuts and optional raisins.

Pour batter into prepared pans. Place the pans on a foil-covered cookie sheet and bake for 1 hour, or until the breads test done. Serve warm or cold.

Hint: You can use this recipe for muffins.

*C*hurros

Makes
12 long churros

Churros are a Mexican version of deep-fried doughnuts. You can use an electric deep fryer or a deep frying pan and 2 inches of oil.

You will need a pastry tube or a cookie press. I find using the tube is simplest. I insert a large star metal tip into the end.

1 tablespoon sugar
2 tablespoons softened butter
1¼ cups water
Pinch of salt (optional)
1 cup flour
2 eggs
Powdered sugar for dusting

Use a heavy saucepan. Combine the sugar, butter, water, and salt. Bring to a boil. Remove pan from heat and quickly add the flour, all at once, using a heavy wooden spoon. Stir until the mixture is smooth and pulls away from the sides of the pan.

Add eggs, one at a time, beating well after each egg is added. Heat the oil to 400° on a candy thermometer. Spoon mixture into the pastry tube and pipe batter into the oil. Make each churro at least 3 inches long.

Fry until golden brown, turning the churros once. Drain on paper towels. Sprinkle with powdered sugar and serve warm.

Hint: Churros get stale in a hurry so don't prepare these in advance.

Sopapillas

Makes
36

I first tasted these fried treats in New Mexico and I was hooked. You can use vegetable shortening to make these instead of lard, but they are not nearly as delicious.

Sopapillas need to be fried and eaten immediately. Sprinkle a little cinnamon-sugar on the tops as you eat them right out of the fryer.

4 tablespoons lard
4 cups flour
1 teaspoon salt
2 teaspoons baking powder
4 eggs
1 cup sugar
Water or milk
Cinnamon-sugar for dusting

Mix together lard, flour, salt, and baking powder until crumbly. Add eggs, sugar, and enough water or milk to make a medium dough. Knead for a few turns and let rest 30 minutes.

Roll out to ¼ inch thickness and cut into wedges. Fry in hot oil, turning each sopapilla once to brown on both sides. Roll the fried goodies in cinnamon and sugar.

Corn Fritters

**Makes
6**

This is an old-fashioned treat, simple and memorable. It does require deep-fat frying. I've got a little tiny fryer. I save the oil after each use and store it in a tightly sealed jar to reuse. I've been told that lard and bear fat make the best frying agents. I'll never know because I use canola oil.

1 (15.25-ounce) can corn
1½ cups flour
1 tablespoon baking powder
Pinch of salt
1 egg, beaten
1 cup milk

Drain corn. Mix flour and baking powder; add salt, egg, and milk and mix until just moistened.

Heat oil to 375°. Drop batter by the tablespoonful into hot oil. Fry for a few minutes, until golden brown.

Drain on paper towels and serve.

Fruit Fritters

Follow directions for Corn Fritters, but substitute 2 cups peeled tart apples, or 2 sliced bananas, or whatever fruit is in season for the corn.

DREAMY PUDDINGS AND MOUSSES

Homey and old-fashioned, pudding is one of my ideal comfort foods. At the other end of the spectrum, rich, luxurious mousse evokes thoughts of romantic, candlelit dinners.

In this chapter you'll find recipes to suit every occasion. To end an elegant evening with international flair, serve sophisticated crème brûlée or arrange a decorative plate of cheese-filled blintzes. You may even want to impress your guests with a soufflé—they'll never guess how simple it was to make.

If you're in the mood for something more cozy, you'll want to turn to the recipes for bread pudding and rice pudding. And for holiday gatherings, nothing rounds out a traditional feast better than steamed plum pudding. You're sure to enjoy the range of recipes offered in the following pages.

Bread Pudding

Serves
12

Bread pudding is old-fashioned, a fabulous way to get rid of stale bread, and elegant enough to serve at a brunch or a potluck dinner. It seems to make everyone happy.

6 eggs, well beaten
1 cup sugar
2 cups light cream
1 stick butter, melted
1 tablespoon vanilla
1 large French or egg bread, broken into pieces
1 teaspoon cinnamon
1 cup crushed pineapple
1 cup raisins, soaked and drained
1 jar Bing cherries, drained, optional

Preheat oven to 350°. Butter a 9 x 13-inch baking pan or a large ceramic baking dish.

Beat eggs with the sugar, cream, butter, and vanilla; pour this mixture over the bread cubes. Stir until bread is moistened. Sprinkle cinnamon over mixture; add pineapple and raisins. Stir in cherries if you are using them.

Press mixture into the pan. Bake 30 to 40 minutes, or until the pudding is set. Serve hot. Serve additional cream to pour over the pudding, or serve with Maple Walnut Sauce (page 77).

Fudge Bread Pudding

Serves
12

2 cups semisweet chocolate chips, or 10 ounces semisweet chocolate
1 stick butter
½ cup sugar
2 cups light cream
4 eggs, well beaten
1 tablespoon vanilla
8 slices white or egg bread, broken into cubes

Preheat oven to 325°. Butter and flour a 6-cup baking dish.

Combine chocolate, butter, and sugar in a saucepan and cook over low heat, stirring constantly, until everything is melted together. Stir until smooth; set aside to cool. Add the cream.

Whisk in eggs and vanilla; fold in the bread. Pour into the prepared pan. Place pan in a larger pan and put both in the oven. Pour 2 inches of hot water into the larger pan and allow the pudding to steam for 40 minutes, or until it is firm in the center.

Serve warm with vanilla ice cream or whipped topping. Take it to a potluck and you will be the star of the show.

Rice Pudding

Serves
12

This is a replica of a fabulous rice pudding I ate at a kosher deli on New York's lower East Side. It has a custard over the creamy rice.

4 large eggs
½ cup sugar
1 teaspoon vanilla
1 cup cream
2 cups milk
1½ cups cooked rice

Preheat oven to 350°. Butter a 2-quart baking dish.

Combine eggs and sugar; add remaining ingredients. Pour mixture into the prepared pan. Bake 1 hour and 15 minutes, or until the pudding is set and golden brown on top.

Serve warm. Embellish with heavy cream.

Hint: You can add raisins, cinnamon, lemon, or orange if you prefer. Or eat this rice pudding just as it is—perfect.

Rice Pudding with Raisins

Serves
12

Delicious, nutritious, and old-fashioned, rice pudding makes a great treat on those days when someone in your family needs a lift.

½ cup uncooked rice
1 cup water
3 eggs, slightly beaten
½ cup sugar
2 teaspoons vanilla
Pinch of salt
2½ cups scalded milk
½ cup raisins, soaked and drained
Sprinkle of cinnamon

Preheat oven to 350°. Butter a 1½-quart baking dish; set aside.

Stir the rice and water into a saucepan. Heat to boiling. Reduce heat and simmer for 15 minutes, or until all the water is absorbed.

Blend the eggs, sugar, vanilla, and salt; gradually add the scalded milk. Mix together with the rice and raisins and pour into buttered baking dish. Sprinkle with cinnamon.

Place the baking dish in a baking pan and put both into the oven. Pour very hot water into the pan—about an inch deep, creating a bain-marie.

Bake pudding about 1 hour, until golden. Serve hot or cold with cream.

Steamed Plum Pudding

**Serves
12**

Steamed pudding resembles canned brown bread in texture. Heavy and moist, it is an elegant dessert to serve after a holiday meal. You can prepare this in a clean, empty two-pound coffee can.

2 cups prunes, soaked, drained, and blended in a food processor
½ cup light molasses
⅓ cup hot water
1 teaspoons baking soda
1½ cups flour

Spray a clean coffee can with vegetable spray. Combine all the ingredients; stir together until smooth. Pour mixture into the coffee can and seal tightly with foil. Place the can in a deep pan with a metal rack on the bottom. Pour enough hot water into the pan so that the water comes to the top of the batter in the can.

Bring water to a gentle boil, cover the pot, and steam for 1½ hours, or until the pudding tests done. Be careful to keep the water at a very slow boil and replace the water as it evaporates.

When the pudding appears to be solid, invert it onto a serving plate. Serve hot with whipped cream, whipped topping, or with Rum Sauce (page 69).

Steamed Pumpkin Pudding

Serves
12

The filament in my oven actually exploded, and until I could get replacement parts, I practiced making steamed puddings. If you like a heavy, moist cake, this is for you. It's great for gift giving and stays fresh for weeks wrapped in foil.

1 cup dark brown sugar, tightly packed
½ cup sugar
1 stick butter, at room temperature
1 teaspoon salt, optional
1 teaspoon cinnamon
2 large eggs, beaten
1 cup chopped walnuts or pecans
2 cups flour
1½ teaspoons baking powder
¼ teaspoon baking soda
1 cup canned pumpkin, mashed
¾ cup cream
½ cup raisins, soaked and drained
1 teaspoon rum extract, or 1 tablespoon rum, optional

Butter a clean 2-pound coffee can; set aside. Using a mixer, combine the sugars, butter, salt, and cinnamon. Add eggs; beat until well mixed. Combine dry ingredients and add alternately with the mashed pumpkin and the cream. Add raisins and, if desired, the rum flavoring or rum.

Pour batter into coffee can or mold. Seal the can tightly with foil and steam according to the directions for Steamed Plum Pudding on page 220.

Remove the can from the water bath and let cool for a few minutes. Invert can onto a serving platter. Dust with powdered sugar.

Hint: If you prefer a spicy cake, add ½ teaspoon ginger and ½ teaspoon nutmeg.

Unbaked Soufflé

Serves
6

This unbaked soufflé is infinitely easy to prepare and never fails. Well, almost never . . .

¼ cup water
⅓ cup creme de cacao, or favorite liqueur
1 envelope unflavored gelatin
⅔ cup brown sugar, tightly packed
1 cup semisweet chocolate chips, melted and cooled
4 eggs, separated
Pinch of salt
1 cup heavy cream

Prepare a 6-cup baking dish. Combine the water and liqueur in a saucepan. Sprinkle gelatin over the liquid. Add ⅓ cup of brown sugar; stir over low heat until everything is dissolved. Add chocolate and stir until well blended. Remove from heat and allow to cool for 5 minutes. Stir in egg yolks, one at a time.

Beat egg whites until very foamy; gradually beat in the second ⅓ cup brown sugar. Beat until stiff.

Beat heavy cream until stiff. Fold cream, chocolate mixture, and egg whites together using a spoon or the side of your hand.

Pour mixture into prepared soufflé dish or bowl and refrigerate 4 hours or overnight.

Easy Chocolate Mousse

**Serves
12 to 18**

Magnifique!

6 eggs, separated
1 cup powdered sugar
1 tablespoon vanilla
2 cups heavy cream
2 ounces semisweet chocolate, melted and cooled
2 ounces unsweetened chocolate, melted and cooled

Prepare a mold for the mousse. Use a 6-cup baking dish around which
you have placed a foil collar that is 2 inches taller than the dish.

Using a mixer, beat the egg whites until very foamy. Add ½ cup
powdered sugar and beat until stiff. (If you beat the egg whites first,
you don't have to clean the bowl or the mixer blade.)

Beat egg yolks until very thick and lemon colored. Add vanilla. In a
separate bowl, beat cream until very foamy. Add second ½ cup powdered sugar and continue beating until stiff.

Fold together the egg whites, the egg yolks, and the sweet whipped
cream. Pour ⅓ of mixture into the prepared mold and chill until set.

Fold melted semisweet chocolate into ⅓ of the mousse and pour it
on top of the white mousse; chill. Fold unsweetened chocolate into the
remaining ⅓ mousse and pour it on top. Cover mousse with foil and
allow to chill at least 24 hours. Invert the mousse onto a serving platter
and garnish.

Tri-color Mousse

Serves
12

A layer of white mousse crowns this three-color mousse creation. You have seen it in patisseries selling for $25 or more. Now you can make it yourself. It takes patience but not a great deal of expertise.

If you have a favorite mousse recipe, use it. The secret is to melt 2 ounces of semisweet chocolate in the microwave and let it cool. Fold it into ⅓ of the mousse. Melt 2 more ounces of unsweetened chocolate in the microwave and fold it into the second ⅓ of the mousse.

Pour first ⅓ of the mousse into a lightly buttered cake pan, 8 or 9 inches across and 3 inches deep. A springform is fine. Refrigerate until set. Pour the semisweet chocolate mousse on top of the white mousse and refrigerate until set.

Pour the remaining dark mousse on the top. Cover the pan with foil and refrigerate for at least 24 hours. If you used a 3-inch deep pan, dip the bottom of the pan in hot water for a minute to release the mousse and invert it onto a serving plate. Garnish with fruit.

This is truly elegant.

*W*hite Chocolate Mousse

Serves
12

Serve this mousse in a pool of chocolate sauce.

6 ounces white chocolate, or 1 cup white chocolate chips
½ cup (8 tablespoons) warm milk
1 (3.4-ounce) package unflavored gelatin
1 tablespoon vanilla
2 egg whites
1 cup whipping cream

Chop the white chocolate and put it in the top of a double boiler with 6 tablespoons of warm milk. Heat until chocolate is melted; stir until smooth. Set aside to cool.

Soften gelatin in the remaining 2 tablespoons of milk; stir until dissolved. Stir gelatin and vanilla into the chocolate mixture until smooth. Cool to room temperature.

Beat egg whites until stiff. Fold egg whites into the chocolate mixture gently. Fold whipped cream into the egg white-chocolate mixture.

Pour mousse into a mold or bowl and chill at least 2 hours.

Hint: This is elegant spooned into tall flute glasses. Serve with fresh fruit.

Crème Brûlée

**Serves
6**

This is known as *crème brûlée* in France and as *flan* in Spanish-speaking countries. By any name, this custard is delicious.

Caramel

12 caramels, unwrapped
¼ cup milk

In a small heavy saucepan, melt caramels and milk together. Or, eliminate this step and use 6 tablespoons of the apple-dipping caramel you can find in the produce department of your supermarket. Spoon about 1 tablespoon of caramel mixture into the bottoms of six 6-ounce custard cups. Or use an 8-inch flan pan or a round baking dish.

Custard

4 eggs
2 cups milk
⅓ cup sugar
Pinch of salt

Mix all the custard ingredients together. Pour the sweet custard mixture over the caramel. Set the cups or pan in a shallow baking dish. Place the baking dish in the oven and fill with hot water to a depth of 1 inch.

Bake 30 to 40 minutes, or until the center is nearly set. Serve warm or chilled. Just before serving, invert the custard cups onto separate plates (or a platter if you've used a flan pan or baking dish).

European Crepes

Makes
18

Crepes are simple to make and require only a little skill. They can be used in many ways—from desserts to entrées.

1 ¾ cups flour
1 cup milk
4 eggs
¾ cup water
1 tablespoon vegetable oil

Place the flour into a bowl. Make a well in the center of the flour and add the milk. Whisk together flour and milk and stir until very smooth. Add the eggs, water, and oil.

Lightly coat a crepe pan or a heavy 8-inch frying pan with butter or oil. I apply the shortening with a paper towel and, over medium heat, add 2 to 3 tablespoons of batter to the pan. Swirl batter in the pan until it covers the bottom of the pan; cook this thin crepe about 15 seconds on each side, until it is lightly browned. Use your fingertips to gently lift the crepe and turn it to brown both sides.

Re-butter the pan after every few crepes to prevent them from sticking.

Hint: These can be prepared a week in advance and stored in a tightly sealed plastic container in your refrigerator.

Blintzes

Mix together 1 cup of farmer cheese and 2 eggs and fill the crepes with this cheese mixture. Chill the filled crepes for several hours and fry them in clarified butter after they are chilled. Instant blintzes.

Extra-Elegant Desserts

This chapter is devoted to a collection of spectacular desserts that are perfect for capping off special occasions. These are the sophisticated and slightly exotic sweets that you may have gazed at longingly through bakery windows or have seen only on the movie screen.

Now, with the help of the following recipes, you can make trifle, baked Alaska, petits fours, tiramisù, and many other decadent desserts in your own kitchen. While a few of these recipes take some extra planning and patience, you'll still be surprised at how easy it is to create these fancy favorites.

Don't hesitate to show off your culinary talent the next time you create an extra-elegant dessert—serve it with a flourish, step back, and take a bow!

Apple Strudel

Makes
72 small or 48
large servings

I have fond childhood memories of strudel. Making the dough was definitely an intense labor of love. There were usually two or three women who were involved in pulling the dough into a huge thin sheet over a dining room table covered with a white cloth sheet.

This recipe is simplified considerably by starting out with prepared filo dough. Be sure to read the directions printed on the box for handling filo dough before starting to work this recipe. You could also use frozen puff pastry dough.

1 pound filo dough, frozen
3 pounds tart apples, peeled,
　　cored, and diced
½ cup raisins, which have been
　　soaked in hot water and
　　drained
1 cup chopped pecans
1 cup sugar

½ teaspoon cinnamon
2 tablespoons lemon juice
1 tablespoon grated lemon peel
½ cup dry bread crumbs
1 egg, slightly beaten, plus 1
　　tablespoon water
Powdered sugar for dusting

Preheat the oven to 400°. Moisten a jelly roll pan (or cookie sheet with sides) with water and shake off the excess. Thaw the frozen filo dough according to the directions on the box.

Combine the apples, drained raisins, nuts, sugar, cinnamon, lemon juice, and lemon peel and mix together. Set aside.

Roll the filo dough into a 10 x 15-inch rectangle, and sprinkle the pastry with the bread crumbs. Leave a 2-inch border on the edges and spread the apple-nut mixture on one long side of the pastry. Roll the filo dough with the filling and place it seam side down on the pan.

Brush the top of the pastry roll with the egg wash and cut diagonal steam vents every inch. Reduce the oven temperature to 350°. Place the strudel in the oven and bake 30 to 40 minutes, or until it is golden brown. Dust with powdered sugar. This is fabulous served warm but still delicious served cold.

Hint: If you know a friendly bakery, you may be able to purchase fresh puff pastry or filo dough from them.

Caramel Torte with Nuts

Serves
12 to 18

This elegant dessert is made simple by using prepared piecrusts, available in the dairy section of most supermarkets.

1½ cups sugar
⅓ cup honey
½ cup water
3½ cups chopped walnuts or pecans
1 stick butter, cut into small cubes
1 cup milk

You will need an 11-inch tart pan with the bottom removed. Place the outer ring of the pan onto a lightly greased cookie sheet.

Preheat oven to 425°. Fit half of the piecrust into the tart ring, allowing about ½ inch of the crust to hang over the top of the ring. Set aside.

Using a saucepan, combine sugar, honey, and water; bring to a boil and cover. Continue to boil for a few minutes and remove cover. Allow mixture to cook until it is a caramel color. Remove from heat and stir in the nuts together with butter cubes. Add milk. Work quickly.

Return pan to heat and continue to cook for 15 minutes, stirring occasionally. Pour the filling into the prepared pastry. Cover the mixture with the remaining crust dough, pressing tightly to seal the top and bottom layers of crust. Cut several slits in the top pastry to allow steam to escape while baking.

Bake the torte 20 minutes. Remove from oven and cool several hours.

Glaze

1 stick sweet butter
1 cup semisweet chocolate chips

Melt butter and chocolate chips together in the microwave. Cool a little.

When torte is completely cooled, invert it onto a large serving plate. Remove the tart ring and glaze the torte with chocolate using a spatula. Refrigerate torte after it has been glazed for a few hours—to make cutting easier.

Baklava

Makes
72

Baklava looks mysterious, exotic, and complicated. The hardest part is separating the filo dough sheets, but if you follow the directions printed on the filo dough box you should have little or no difficulty.

Syrup

5 cups sugar
3 cups water
Juice of 1 lemon
1 teaspoon cinnamon
2 tablespoons honey

Combine all the ingredients in a heavy saucepan and cook until medium thick. Cool.

Filling

2 pounds chopped walnuts, almonds, macadamia nuts
1 cup sugar
2 teaspoons cinnamon
½ teaspoon nutmeg
1 pound butter, melted
2 pounds filo pastry sheets

Grind the nuts and mix with the sugar and spices. You can use a processor with a metal blade.

Grease a cookie sheet that has sides with melted butter. Preheat oven to 325°. Butter each sheet of filo dough before using it. Use your fingers or a pastry brush.

Stack baklava in this manner:

10 sheets buttered filo dough, directly onto the cookie sheet
½ nut mix, spread on top of filo dough
10 sheets buttered filo dough
½ nut mix, spread on top of filo dough

Chill baklava at least 1 hour. Mark baklava into small squares, then into diamond shapes before baking it.

Bake 1½ hours, or until lightly browned. Remove from oven and pour syrup on top.

Hint: If you eliminate the syrup, roll the dough, and then slice it, you have a version of strudel that is delicious.

Cream Puffs

Makes 36

The fancy name for tiny cream puffs filled with cream and dipped in chocolate is *profiteroles*. They are elegant and simple to make.

¾ cup water
½ teaspoon salt
⅓ cup unsalted butter, cut into small pieces
¾ cup plus 2 tablespoons flour
4 eggs
1 egg and pinch of salt for glaze

Preheat oven to 400°. Spray a cookie sheet with nonstick spray or cover it with parchment paper.

Combine water, salt, and butter in a large pan. Bring mixture just to a boil. Add flour to the water-butter mixture all at once and beat with a wooden spoon.

Remove mixture from heat; continue to beat until it forms a ball. Return to very low heat and continue stirring for about 1 minute, or until the dough dries out somewhat.

Remove from heat. Beat eggs in one at a time, using a wooden spoon. The batter will become shiny. Place a metal tip with a large round opening into the bottom of a pastry bag. Press the dough out onto a cookie sheet about an inch apart, or drop pastry by the tablespoonful onto the prepared cookie sheet.

Glaze the puffs before baking. Mix an egg with a pinch of salt added and carefully brush onto the tops of the puffs. Gently press down on each puff with the tines of a fork to make a crossover pattern.

Bake 20 to 25 minutes, until the puffs are rounded and golden. Remove cookie sheet from the oven and make a small slit in the side of each puff to release the steam. Allow the puffs to cool completely.

When the puffs are cool, split them in half and fill them with whipped cream, ice cream, custard, or pudding.

Eclairs

If you use a pastry tube and pipe a log shape about 3 inches long on the cookie sheet, you will have an eclair shape. Proceed with instructions for cream puffs.

Cream Puff Pastry Ring

Serves
12

Easy and exquisite. Use the recipe for Cream Puffs and proceed as follows:

Use a lightly oiled cookie sheet and a ⅝-inch metal tip inserted into a pastry bag. Pipe out an 8-inch circle of pastry, and another circle on top of it, and one beside it to make the ring full. You can use a spoon to even out the edges.

Add a pinch of salt to 1 beaten egg and brush the glaze onto the pastry ring. Bake the ring at 350° until brown, 30 to 35 minutes.

Slit the ring to release steam and cool. Slice the ring in half after it has cooled, maintaining the circle. Fill the center of the ring with custard, pudding, ice cream, or flavored whipped cream. Layer strawberries or sliced fruit around the outer circle of the ring. Replace the top half of the ring.

Drizzle chocolate sauce over the top. Dip sugar cubes in brandy, light the cubes with a match, turn out the lights, and have a glorious flaming dessert.

Cream Puff Swans

Makes
24 to 36

These are dazzling floating on a pool of chocolate sauce. You've seen them in expensive patisseries and in elegant hotel dining rooms—now you can make them yourself. The instructions may sound complicated, but are really quite simple. You will be thrilled with the results.

Follow instructions for making Cream Puffs. After batter has been prepared, you will need a pastry bag with a plastic connector to change tips, or you can use two pastry bags. One metal tip should have a round opening at least ½ inch wide and one should have an opening of about ¼ inch. (These can be purchased at a bakery supply store or a gourmet shop that carries baking equipment.)

Preheat oven to 350°. Lightly oil two cookie sheets or cover with parchment paper.

Prepare a batch of cream puff pastry and put the dough into the pastry tube. Squeeze out ovals of pastry dough about 2 inches across onto the prepared cookie sheet using the tip with the large opening. Change the tip and pipe out a shape which will serve as the neck and head of the swan, an S shape. (Continued on next page.)

Use a separate cookie sheet for the bodies and the necks. Bake the necks 10 to 15 minutes, or until golden brown; bake bodies 30 to 35 minutes. Cut a slit in the cream puff body to release steam; allow the puffs to cool completely before cutting in half horizontally.

Cut the top half of the cream puff into halves. These will form the wings of the swans. Fill the bottom half of the cream puff with whipped cream or custard and insert the baked S-shaped pastry for the head and neck of the swan. Insert the pieces you cut in half for the wings.

Float the swans in a pool of melted chocolate.

Bananas Flambé

Serves
8

Also known as Bananas Foster, this is a dessert you served in ultra-posh restaurants. It's very sweet and, served over vanilla ice cream, it is simple and dazzling.

You'll want to use a chafing dish so you can prepare this *au table, comme le maitre d'.*

½ cup brown sugar, tightly packed
½ stick sweet butter, at room temperature
½ teaspoon cinnamon
4 bananas, peeled, sliced in half lengthwise
½ cup dark rum
1 quart vanilla ice cream

Use a heavy saucepan or a chafing dish. Combine sugar, butter, and cinnamon. Heat until well mixed and the butter is melted. Add bananas and cook until they just start to soften. Add rum and heat thoroughly.

Place the banana halves on dessert plates and cover with ice cream. Now the dramatic part: Using a long match, ignite the sauce. After the flames have died away, spoon the sauce over the ice cream.

Kahlua Chocolate Charlotte Malakoff

**Serves
12 to 18**

This requires no baking—the preparation is extremely simple and the result is beautiful. A terrific way to use leftover whipped cream frosting, this dessert is totally elegant. It can be made in a glass bowl with high sides or a springform pan.

¾ cup Kahlua
½ cup water
24 ladyfingers
2 sticks sweet butter, at room temperature
1 cup powdered sugar
1 tablespoon almond extract
1⅓ cups ground almonds
4 ounces (½ cup) semisweet chocolate chips, melted and cooled
2 cups cream

Butter a 10-inch springform pan and set it aside. Mix together ½ cup Kahlua and the water. Dip ladyfingers in this mixture and stand them against the buttered sides and bottom of the springform pan. Chill.

Beat together butter and sugar until light and fluffy. Add almond extract, ground almonds, and melted chocolate; beat until smooth.

Whip the cream until it is stiff. Add the remaining ¼ cup Kahlua; gently fold into the chocolate-butter mixture. Scoop mixture into the springform; chill at least 4 hours before serving.

Hint: When you are ready to remove the springform pan, wrap a tea towel that has been soaked in hot water around the pan for a few minutes. Release the spring, use a spatula to remove the bottom plate, and serve.

Baked Alaska

Serves
12 to 18

This dessert is carried out into the darkened ballrooms of elegant cruise ships after the final gala dinner. The waiters carry this flaming dessert high in the air while singing "Auld Lang Syne." Brings a tear to the eye and a lump to the throat. Impress your guests with this easy dessert.

1 (8-inch square) pan of brownies or cake
1 quart spumoni or any multicolored ice cream, packed in a rectangular
  box
6 egg whites
½ cup extra-fine sugar

Bake the cake or brownies. Cool completely and freeze until solid, at least 1 hour. Place the block of ice cream directly on the brownies, allowing about 1 inch of cake to extend beneath the ice cream. Return cake and ice cream to the freezer and freeze until very hard—up to 6 weeks.

Preheat oven to 500°. Using a mixer, beat the egg whites until very frothy. Slowly add sugar and beat until stiff to create a meringue.

Remove the ice cream and brownie block from the freezer. Cover the top and sides with the meringue.

Place baked Alaska in a hot oven for 5 to 10 minutes, or until the meringue starts to brown. Remove the dessert from the oven and serve immediately.

Hint: If you wish, soak several cubes of sugar in brandy and light the top of the baked Alaska. Or use candles. Very impressive!

Ice Cream Bombe

Serves
18 to 24

This will bring an explosion of admiration when it is served. You can prepare this long in advance and keep it frozen until serving time.

4 quarts ice cream, any flavors and colors that will look beautiful when sliced

Use a 4-quart bowl or a large gelatin mold. Freeze the bowl or mold before beginning assembly of the bombe.

Allow one quart of the ice cream to stand at room temperature for about 10 minutes, or until soft enough to handle with a spoon or your hands. Press softened ice cream into the chilled mold, covering the bottom and sides of the mold.

Return mold to the freezer until the ice cream is frozen solid. Repeat process using another flavor of softened ice cream, pressing the new flavor against the bottom and sides of the mold. Return mold to the freezer until it is frozen solid.

Repeat the process using a third flavor of ice cream; return mold to freezer. Fill the remaining space with the fourth flavor of ice cream.

Return mold to freezer until serving time. At serving time, carefully dip the entire mold in very warm water, making sure that none of the water goes over the top. Invert onto a large serving platter; garnish with fresh flowers or fruit. Slice and serve.

Hint: Pass a warm jar of Chocoholics ChocolateButter for your guests to spoon over the bombe.

Trifle

Serves
18 to 24

Trifle is simple to prepare, dazzling to serve, and a great way to dispose of leftover cake. This is the thing to do with cakes that flop—thanks Nan!

Feel free to change fruit and the layering. Use the custard of your choice: make your own or use a package mix. The Irish version, according to an acquaintance, is to pour cooled liquid gelatin over the cake.

3 cups whipping cream
1 (7-ounce) box French vanilla instant pudding
½ cup powdered sugar
1 pound cake, or 4 cups cake scraps
¼ cup liqueur
½ cup water
3 large bananas, sliced
1 pint fresh raspberries
3 fresh peaches, sliced
1 cup raspberry jam

You will need a deep glass bowl, about 6 inches deep and 8 to 10 inches across. Whip the cream until frothy. Fold in pudding mix. Add powdered sugar and beat until stiff. Refrigerate.

Slice the pound cake into slices about the size of ladyfingers. Mix liqueur and water. Dip each slice carefully in the liqueur-water mixture. Cover the bottom of the bowl with some of the sliced pound cake.

Drizzle some raspberry jam over the ladyfingers. Spoon fruit over the ladyfingers and spread about 1 inch of whipped cream over the top of the fruit.

Continue making layers alternately of pound cake, jam, fruit, and whipped cream until you have filled the bowl.

Refrigerate the trifle until serving time. Spoon into long-stemmed glasses; garnish with any remaining fruit and whipped cream.

Petit Fours

It requires some work to create these delicacies, but the results are very impressive.

3 eggs
½ cup extra-fine sugar
1 teaspoon vanilla
¾ cup flour, sifted
2 tablespoons butter, melted and cooled
1 cup apricot preserves, mixed with 1 tablespoon warm water

Preheat oven to 350°. Butter and flour a 10 x 14-inch cake pan or a cookie sheet with sides.

Combine eggs and sugar in a medium-sized mixing bowl. Place the bowl over boiling water until the egg-sugar mixture is skin temperature. Using a mixer, whip the egg-sugar mixture until it has doubled in volume.

Add vanilla. Fold in the flour. Mix in the melted butter. Pour batter into prepared pan and bake until set. You can leave the cake in the pan and freeze it for an hour, pan and all. This will make it easier to cut the cake into squares.

Cut the cake into 1-inch squares and brush away the crumbs. Brush melted apricot jam onto tops of cake cubes. Discard any chunks of apricots in the preserves. If you like, press two squares together to make a larger petit four.

Place the cake cubes on a rack over wax paper and pour melted chocolate or pastel-colored icing over the tops. Decorate with fruit or nuts, or pipe with melted chocolate.

Easy Petit Fours

Use white cake mix and the Magic Cake Mix recipe (page 20), omitting egg yolks. Spread the batter on the bottom of a lightly greased and floured cookie sheet that has sides. Bake at 350° until the cake is lightly browned, about 15 minutes.

Cut the cake into squares and layer each petit four with apricot jam. Freeze the squares until they are easy to handle.

Microwave a can of ready-to-spread frosting for 45 seconds; stir it until smooth. Dip petit fours into the melted frosting using a fondue fork. Set the frosted cubes on a wire cake rack over wax paper so you will be able to reuse the frosting that drips off the cake cubes.

Place a candied violet on top of the mark made by the fondue fork . They will be exquisite.

Tiramisù

This has recently become a very popular dessert. The original recipe calls for mascarpone cheese, which resembles cream cheese whipped to the consistency of whipped cream. This is difficult to find in remote areas like Humboldt County, California. I have designed this recipe using cream cheese in place of the mascarpone.

2 (8-ounce) packages cream cheese, at room temperature, cut into
    pieces
2 cups sugar
4 tablespoons milk
4 teaspoons vanilla
4 tablespoons brandy
3½ cups whipping cream
2½ cups strong coffee
1 package ladyfingers
½ cup cocoa powder

Use a mixer to beat the cream cheese, sugar, and milk together until the mixture is very light and fluffy. Blend in vanilla and brandy. Transfer this mixture to another bowl.

Whip the cream until it is stiff and carefully fold it into the cream cheese mixture. Cover and refrigerate for about 1 hour. This can be prepared several days in advance.

Pour coffee into a shallow dish. Dip the ladyfingers into the coffee, turning to dampen, but not soak, both sides. Arrange the ladyfingers on the bottom and sides of a 9 x 12-inch serving dish. Pour in the cheese mixture.

Put cocoa in a small strainer or into a sugar shaker and dust the top of the dessert evenly. Refrigerate. Spoon the tiramisù into serving bowls or tall wine glasses.

Hint: You can replace the ladyfingers with slices of pound cake or butter cookies.

Fruit Compote

Serves
8

This simple dish is lovely served with a meal or as a dessert. It is a Jewish tradition for holiday dinners.

¼ cup golden raisins
1 pound dried mixed fruit
1 cup warm water
1 cup white wine
½ cup sugar, optional
1 teaspoon cinnamon
1 lemon, juice and rind

Preheat oven to 350°. Combine the fruit, water, and wine in a baking dish and marinate the dried fruit for 1 hour. Stir in the sugar, if desired. Add the cinnamon, lemon juice, and rind.

Cover the dish with foil and bake 1 hour. Serve warm—plain or with sour cream or whipped cream.

Amaretto Fruit Compote

Serves
6

You can use your favorite liqueur and vary the fruit for this simple but elegant dessert. Perfect after a heavy dinner or on a summer night.

1 small can frozen orange juice concentrate
2 pints fresh strawberries
8 fresh peaches
Sugar to taste
3 tablespoons fresh lemon juice
½ cup amaretto, or favorite liqueur

Remove orange juice concentrate from freezer and thaw completely. Hull and wash the strawberries and dry them on toweling.

Peel peaches, remove the pits, and slice into quarters. Place the fruit in a shallow glass bowl and sprinkle with sugar and fresh lemon juice to taste.

Stir the liqueur and orange juice together. Pour over the fruits; stir gently. Cover and refrigerate for no more than 2 hours.

Serve in long-stemmed glasses.

Hint: Because the fruit will not keep more than a few hours without turning dark and soggy, make this just before your guests arrive and serve it within 2 hours of preparation.

Index